Let Go of Clutter

ALSO BY HARRIET SCHECHTER

Conquering Chaos at Work: Strategies for Managing Disorganization and the People Who Cause It

More Time for Sex: The Organizing Guide for Busy Couples

LET GO OF CLUTTER

Harriet Schechter

Illustrations by Bella Silverstein

McGraw-Hill

New York   San Francisco   Washington, D.C.   Auckland   Bogotá
Caracas   Lisbon   London   Madrid   Mexico City   Milan
Montreal   New Delhi   San Juan   Singapore
Sydney   Tokyo   Toronto

McGraw-Hill

A Division of The McGraw·Hill Companies

8 9 0   DOC/DOC   0 9 8 7 6 5 4 3

ISBN 0-07-135122-1

This book was set in 11/16 Baskerville
by Impressions Book and Journal Services, Inc.

Printed and bound by R. R. Donnelley & Sons Company.

This publication is designed to provide accurate and authoritative information in regard to the subject matter covered. It is sold with the understanding that the publisher is not engaged in rendering legal, accounting, or other professional service. If legal advice or other expert assistance is required, the services of a competent professional person should be sought.

—From a declaration of principles jointly adopted by a committee
of the American Bar Association and a committee of publishers.

 This book is printed on recycled, acid-free paper containing a minimum of 50% recycled de-inked fiber.

McGraw-Hill books are available at special quantity discounts to use as premiums and sales promotions, or for use in corporate training programs. For more information, please write to the Director of Special Sales, Professional Publishing, McGraw-Hill, Two Penn Plaza, New York, NY 10121. Or contact your local bookstore.

For my sister
Janet
and my brother
Stuart

Contents

● ●

Acknowledgments

● ●

Gratitude is one of the few things we should never let go of or stop accumulating. I have unending gratitude for the assistance, support, and kindness of all the wonderful people who helped me produce this book.

To begin with, the team at McGraw-Hill has been outstanding. Betsy Brown deserves special thanks because it was she who first suggested that I write a book based on my workshops. Thank you, Betsy, for your vision, perseverance, patience, suggestions, and all you did to make *Let Go of Clutter* a reality. Richard Narramore took over where Betsy left off, and his ability to handle the seemingly endless editorial details gracefully and efficiently is unparalleled. Thanks, Richard, for the smooth transition and for being such a pleasure to work with. Other team members who deserve special mention include Art Director Eileen Kramer, who conjured up the delightful cover design; Production Supervisor Elizabeth Strange, who pulled all the pieces together; Editing Supervisor Patricia Amoroso and copyeditor Frances Koblin, who made sure everything fit just right; and last but not least, Philip Ruppel, for giving this project the green light.

This is my second book with Bella Silverstein, whose illustrations brighten these pages. A true professional is someone who does a great job *and* gets it done on time and within budget, no matter what obstacles pop up. Bella, if I could draw a picture of a true professional, it would look just like you. Thanks for your delightful art, your cheerful attitude, and your exemplary work ethic.

I am indeed fortunate to have my very own Miracle Worker, Marcia Richardson, without whom I would not get much accomplished nor have as much fun doing it. She has been with me through the agony and the ecstasy of creating three books, and has somehow managed to remain unphased through every phase. Thanks, Marcia, for everything.

My husband, Henry, puts up with a lot from me, especially when I'm involved in a book project, yet manages to be unfailingly kind, understanding, helpful, accommodating, and loving. But equal to all that is the fact that he's a great photographer, and always makes me look good in my publicity photos. Henry, I can never thank you enough for everything you do, so please try to think of my nagging as a form of gratitude.

Others whose consistent support I treasure include Donna Cowan, T.R. Fleischer, Bridget Hanley, Sharon Kristensen Demere, Charmaine Gunnell, Ruth Klampert, and Ruth Williams; the late Helen Delany, Queen of Serendipity; all my wonderful clients and the thousands of workshop participants who have helped to make my Letting Go of Clutter course such a success; the San Diego Learning Annex team, especially Debbie Luican, Kathy Lueder, and Deb Ingersoll; and the team at the Margret McBride Literary Agency, in particular Sangeeta Mehta, Kris Sauer, Donna DeGutis and, of course, Margret herself.

My family also deserves a special note of thanks. My brother, Stuart, has been extremely helpful at crucial times; my parents provide endless love and, perhaps unwittingly, great material; and my sister, Janet, along with her husband, Stan, and amazing children, Louis and Irene, are also a source of joy and inspiration.

Thank you, one and all!

HARRIET SCHECHTER

Introduction

● ●

I'll never forget the time I taught my first Letting Go of Clutter workshop.

It was standing room only. Almost 100 people were crammed into a meeting room that had seemed spacious when empty. Quickly it became evident that these people were desperate for answers to their clutter problems. Even before class had officially begun, they were bombarding me with questions like:

"What can I do about the feeling that I can't let go of the clutter?"

"How do I stop letting my mail pile up?"

"What can I do with cards and letters I can't bear to part with?"

"How long do I need to keep tax papers?"

"What can I do to make myself deal with my clutter?"

"How do I clear out the wall-to-wall clutter in my garage?"

"What should I do about all the magazines and newspaper clippings I want to read someday?"

"How can I unclutter my closets and get rid of clothes that are still perfectly good?"

"Is there any way to keep my desk uncluttered?"

And my favorite question, which I was to hear many times over the ensuing years—sometimes expressed quite forcefully:

"Why do we keep all this stuff?!"

I have answered these questions, and many more, in the monthly workshops I've taught since 1988—and now in this book. But don't think the answers came easily. Clutter is difficult to deal with, in part because it's so subjective. One person's clutter is another's treasure, and vice versa. Clutter is relative—and sometimes it's a relative's. That has certainly been true for me.

HOW I GOT THE ANSWERS

I'm the product of a mixed marriage: my mother is a clutterer, and my father isn't. Luckily, I got the best of both worlds. I've always enjoyed putting things in order, and I have compassion for people who are overwhelmed with clutter. Is it any wonder that with these traits, I ended up becoming a professional organizer—and then marrying the most disorganized man in the world? (And no, he wasn't a client, in case you're wondering.)

Long before I officially embarked on my organizing career, I'd been helping family, friends, and coworkers. They'd tell me, "You're so good at this—someone should pay you to do it!" (Not that they ever offered to, of course. What they really meant was, "Someone else should pay you.") It took me years to realize that they were right.

Eventually I started a company to help others organize and declutter their lives. Since 1986 I have helped thousands of individuals, couples, businesses, and institutions become less cluttered and more productive. In the process, I've learned a tremendous amount from my clients and workshop participants.

The clutter-conquering methods in this book are real-life solutions, tried-and-tested techniques and tips from my years as an organizing consultant. My advice reflects the time I've spent in the clutter trenches with all kinds of wonderful people, in every imaginable situation and line of work—literally from accountants to zookeepers. I've helped doctors and dog trainers, executives and entrepreneurs, housewives and horticulturists, lawyers and librarians, publicists and publishers, salespeople and social workers, teachers and tycoons... and the main thing they've all had in common besides their clutter problem was a strong desire to conquer it.

The anecdotes and quotes from these courageous people are true; the names and certain details have been changed, however, to protect the organizationally impaired.

WHO SHOULD READ THIS BOOK

This book was written for anyone who wants to let go of clutter instead of just reorganizing it.

Let Go of Clutter is for you if:

- You are tired of reorganizing your possessions.
- You want to let go of your clutter, but you don't know how or where to begin.
- You have difficulty letting go of things—clothes, books, papers, or any other kind of material objects.
- You feel overwhelmed by the continual build-up of clutter in your home, your office, your car... your life.
- You are afraid to get rid of stuff because you think that once you do, you'll regret it.

The advice this book contains is geared toward those who are dealing primarily with their own clutter. If you live with or love someone whose clutter concerns you, it is important to accept that you may not be able to help them declutter unless they are willing to be helped. Additional resources for clutter situations involving children and spouses are provided in the Afterword and in Appendix B.

ARE YOU A TRUE PACKRAT?

Over the years I've observed that the people who call me for help or who attend my workshops tend to be either:

1. Basically organized but overwhelmed with clutter
2. Basically disorganized but wanting to get organized
3. Victims of "Packrat Syndrome" (PS)

PS is actually a clinically described condition related to Obsessive-Compulsive Disorder. (About a quarter of the 5 million Americans with Obsessive-Compulsive Disorder exhibit symptoms of hoarding and cluttering.) People with PS insatiably collect and hoard vast quantities of materials that often have little or no perceived value to others. When they try to let go of any of their stuff, the process usually makes them feel bad instead of good; they will often grieve over items they got rid of long ago.

If you identify with category 1 or category 2, the advice in this book may be all you need to help you let go of clutter. If, however, you have PS or care about someone who does, you may need additional assistance—but don't despair! Appendix B includes resources for helping PS sufferers.

WHAT THIS BOOK WILL HELP YOU DO

Let Go of Clutter has two interconnected objectives:

- To give you a painless process for letting go of whatever is cluttering up your life—past and present

- To show you how to overcome future clutter by managing the urge to acquire and accumulate

Note that "to help you get organized" is not on the list. That's because organizing stuff is not the same as letting go of it. What's more, organizing can actually obstruct the letting go process by:

- Giving you a way to put off getting rid of stuff as you endlessly putter with your clutter
- Providing you with a good excuse to buy more stuff (disguised as "organizing supplies")
- Encouraging you to keep too much stuff (Rearranging often enables you to fill up every square inch of storage space. But hey, as long as it all looks organized, it's not clutter—right? Ha.)

This is not an "organizing book" in the sense that it does not focus on storage solutions, product recommendations, or suggestions for how to maximize your space. But this is not an anti-organizing book, either. Far from it. I've included organizing techniques that I know from experience are helpful in the decluttering process. As you'll see, both the first and the last steps of decluttering involve organizing.

DECLUTTERING STEPS

1. **EXCAVATE AND CATEGORIZE:** Round up your clutter, area by area, and group similar items together.
2. **DECIDE AND DIVEST:** Choose what to let go of and what to keep; discard, destroy, or donate/recycle whatever you can live without.
3. **ARRANGE AND SYSTEMATIZE:** Put what's left (and remember, what's left is what's right!) into any order that consistently pleases you or makes your life easier.

● ●

The Topic Is Clutter

The focus of this book is on providing effective methods for letting go of clutter. Therefore, I chose not to clutter it up with certain topics that are often linked to or lumped with clutter, such as overcoming procrastination, perfectionism, and chronic lateness; housekeeping hints; and efficiency tips. While such topics may have relevance, they can also become detours on the path to conquering clutter.

● ●

As you learn to let go of more and more clutter, you may find yourself becoming more organized. (You may find a lot of other things, too. But we'll deal with that later.) This bonus is often a pleasant by-product of the letting-go-of-clutter process. But do keep in mind that it's a by-product, and not the goal. The goal is to let go of clutter—and the more you let go, the less you'll have to organize. That's why *Let Go of Clutter* is mainly about how to choose—confidently, consistently, and without fear of regret—what to jettison. It's about lightening your load, dropping off excess ballast so you can soar up and away. And that's why the techniques covered in the following pages are designed to help you get rid of stuff instead of just putting it all away somewhere... in baskets, boxes, bags, cabinets, closets, containers, and all of the other popular organizer-storage devices.

Getting rid of your existing clutter is an important goal—but it's only part of what this book is about. To really let go of clutter, you also need to know how to let go of future clutter. After all, if you're acquiring stuff faster than you're getting rid of it, you're not going to stay uncluttered for long—as you may have already discovered. (Ever notice how quickly newly emptied drawers and closet space seem to fill up?) That's why the second goal of this book is to show you how to manage your desire to acquire so you can stop being a slave to stuff.

Let the journey begin...

HOW THIS BOOK IS ORGANIZED

Let Go of Clutter is divided into three parts corresponding to your past, present, and future clutter concerns:

Part I: The Past—Understanding Your Clutter Background

Part II: The Present—Dealing with Your Current Clutter

Part III: The Future—Controlling Your Clutter Quota

The top 10 most frequently asked clutter questions are answered throughout these three parts. Other frequently asked clutter questions, along with their answers, are included in the Afterword. The appendixes provide additional resources to help you continue letting go of clutter. For updated information on this topic, visit this book's companion website, www.letgoclutter.com.

THE TOP 10 CLUTTER QUESTIONS— AND WHERE YOU'LL FIND THE ANSWERS

All participants in my Letting Go of Clutter workshops are asked to write down one question about clutter that is of the most concern to them. Since 1988 I've sorted through thousands of these questions, and organized them into representative categories. Here are 10 of the most frequently asked questions and where you'll find the answers in this book.

Q: Why do we keep all this stuff?

A: See Chapter One.

Q: What can I do about the feeling that I can't let go of the clutter?

A: See Chapters One and Two.

Q: What can I do to make myself deal with my clutter?

A: See Chapter Three.

Q: What should I do about all the magazines and newspaper clippings I want to read someday?

A: See Chapter Four.

Q: Is there any way to keep my desk uncluttered?

A: See Chapter Four.

Q: How do I stop letting my mail pile up?

A: See Chapter Four.

Q: How can I unclutter my closets and get rid of clothes that are still perfectly good?

A: See Chapters Five and Seven.

Q: How do I clear out the wall-to-wall clutter in my garage?

A: See Chapter Five.

Q: What can I do with cards and letters I can't bear to part with?

A: See Chapter Six.

Q: How long do I need to keep tax papers?

A: See Chapter Four and Appendix A.

Let Go of Clutter

The Past

● ●

Understanding Your Clutter Background

Why Letting Go Is Hard to Do

● ●

A key step in letting go of clutter is recognizing the forces that influence you to acquire and hold on to stuff. Why? Because knowing what you're up against helps you make better choices.

OVERVIEW

This chapter helps you understand why it seems so hard to let go of clutter. Understanding leads to power—power over the invisible influences that cause you to accumulate and hold on to things. These influences are linked to three clutter contributing factors:

 THE CLUTTER CHROMOSOME—Why you may be biologically wired to acquire and accumulate

 THE CLUTTER COMPULSION—How you are psychologically programmed to hang onto stuff

3 **THE CLUTTER CULTURE**—How you are sociologically influenced to collect clutter endlessly

Why is it so hard to let go of stuff? Because accumulating comes naturally to us, and so the opposite—divesting—feels unnatural.

This answer dawned on me one day while I was feeding a blue jay on my patio. The bird, who visits almost daily, likes to hoard the tidbits I give him. He'll grab offerings from my hand, scurry over to the lawn or a bush, tuck the bounty away under a tuft of grass or a leaf, then hurry back to me for the next treat. I'm sure that if I had nothing to do all day but sit there and feed him, this process would continue around the clock. Because no matter how much he gets, it will never be enough; the bird is programmed to gather and hoard perpetually. Good thing he doesn't have access to credit cards, catalogs, infomercials, and the Internet.

WIRED TO ACQUIRE

My feathered friend's behavior made me think about the fact that the packrat instinct isn't confined to packrats (the rodents, I mean). All kinds of creatures—mollusks, insects, birds, primates, even some dogs and cats—are born with something in their brains that tells them to keep stockpiling stuff. (Perhaps a tiny QVC spokesperson.)

Is it possible that people's brains, too, are biologically wired to acquire and accumulate? Based on my own highly unscientific experiments, I believe it's more than possible. The fact that the elusive "clutter chromosome" has not been found—it was actually misplaced long ago—doesn't mean there isn't plenty of other evidence to support its existence. This seems like good news for anyone who has ever claimed that clutter problems are genetic. Tired of blaming your parents? Now you can blame your primitive ancestors!

Throughout history and prehistory, humankind has been on a relentless quest to acquire more—more food, more territory, more people, more money, more information, more stuff. (Even the expression "less is more" reflects this truth. As trend-tracker Faith Popcorn observed, "What we want now is less. More and more less.") Our methods for getting more have ranged from bartering, buying, and borrowing to stealing, battling, and plundering.

Let me give you just a little food for thought—actually, "foodstuff" for thought. Food was only the first form of stockpileable stuff. When feast or famine was reality, as it was until relatively recently, stockpiling of food was a survival strategy. It's certainly a good thing that our ancestors were programmed to hoard as well as hunt and gather, otherwise the species might have died out. (I suspect the real reason why dinosaurs became extinct is that their food was just way too big and they ran out of storage space.) Unfortunately, however, our biology hasn't caught up with our present reality. It's as though the famine button is stuck in the "on" position while we are in the perma-feast mode. So the hunter has become the hunted: we are possessed by our possessions. We have many more types of stuff than our ancestors ever could have imagined. Who knew?!

"That which you cannot give away, you do not possess. It possesses you." —*Ivern Ball*

My point is this: Overabundance is a natural outgrowth of our basic need to acquire and accumulate. This goes counter to the unchallenged murmurings of the "simplicity police," who use the comparatively simple lifestyle of our great-grandparents as proof that simple is more "natural"; an excess of stuff is therefore unnatural. But this line of reasoning does not take into account the fact that in the past, there was only a limited amount of stuff to be acquired (and no credit cards with which to acquire it). Times, and stuff, have changed—yet people have not. We weren't designed to either deny ourselves or divest ourselves of stuff— just the opposite. So, it's only natural to want to get—and keep getting— more...and more. Letting go of stuff therefore is difficult because it goes against our basic instinct.

Difficult, however, is not the same as impossible. You can learn to counteract the clutter chromosome and override your instinct to acquire and accumulate. That's what this book will teach you to do. But first, we need to confront the other key factors that make it hard to let go of clutter.

● ●
Clutching Clutter?
Are you *literally* afraid to let go of stuff? If you constantly misplace things, perhaps it's because you move from place to place clutching something in your hands that you end up putting down somewhere it doesn't belong. Make a conscious effort to release objects from your grasp, and leave them where they belong.
● ●

COMPELLED TO KEEP CLUTTER

Not only are we biologically wired to acquire stuff, we are also psychologically programmed to hang onto it. I believe our compulsion to keep things is rooted in fear, especially the fear of regret. Because regret is such a painful emotion, we try to avoid it. This fuels one of the biggest excuses for keeping clutter: "Whenever I get rid of something, I end up needing it!" Who hasn't had the experience of getting rid of something— an article of clothing, a book, a piece of furniture, a gadget, whatever— and then suffering pangs of regret later? (Especially when you hear about a similar item getting sold on eBay or the Antiques Roadshow for thousands of dollars.)

GET OVER IT

What happened the last time you got rid of something and then regretted it? (Believe me, it's happened to almost everyone.) You got over it, didn't you? That's what psychologically healthy people do. They get over it, and move on. That doesn't mean you won't occasionally experience a twinge of regret. But you don't let it consume your thoughts and shape your life. However, if you do find yourself grieving over the loss of something that was never alive to begin with, you need more help than I can give you, and I urge you to seek counseling. Life is too short to waste time wallowing in regret. (Please see Appendix B for Packrat Syndrome support resources.)

Until you let go of your regrets, you haven't really let go of your clutter. You may have gotten rid of clutter, but you're still hanging onto it. Your regret has created an invisible chain that keeps you tied to something heavier than an iron ball: your clutter ghosts. Set them free, and you'll free yourself of the fear of regret that holds you back from letting go of more clutter.

The accompanying "Get Over It" worksheet is designed to help you let go of any lingering regrets you may have that might hinder your decluttering efforts.

Completing the "Get Over It" worksheet will most likely help you perceive that either:

- Your regrets are usually a waste of time and a poor excuse for you to keep hanging onto clutter; or
- Your regrets have wisely prevented you from making further regrettable errors in judgment (e.g., divesting yourself of other valuable or meaningful items)

Either way, you've started to become more conscious of the effect your fear of regret may have on the choices you make.

● ●

Replace Regret

Remind yourself that if you get rid of something, you can usually get it again. Most things are replaceable.

● ●

THE "GET OVER IT" WORKSHEET

Instructions: In the first column, write down everything you regret having gotten rid of. (Please limit your list to inanimate items.) In the second column, write next to each item why you regretted, or still regret, getting rid of it. In the third column, describe the result or effect that the regretted choice has had on your life. And in the fourth column, categorize the result or effect as positive, negative, or neutral.

Items I've regretted getting rid of	Why?	What happened as a result?	Was the result positive, negative, or neutral?

FEAR OF REGRET: Your regret has created an invisible chain that keeps you tied to your clutter ghosts.

IT'S YOUR CHOICE

Getting rid of something and regretting it later isn't the only type of clutter-causing regret. There's another one: the regret that you spent money on the thing in the first place. (Anyone who's ever had an expensive, never-worn garment, with the price tag still attached, hanging forlornly in the closet for years knows what I'm talking about.) This can cause you to try to justify your choice subconsciously by holding onto it. See, if you get rid of it, it's like admitting you made a bad choice—horror of horrors, a mistake! And for some people, that possibility is just too painful to acknowledge.

What both types of regret have in common is this: They're a signal that you feel uncomfortable with the choices you've made about what to keep and what to let go of. Part of the process of letting go involves changing your mind, making choices—conscious choices—that are different from the ones you've been making unconsciously. This is, in effect, reprogramming yourself.

As you read this book, you'll learn how to make different choices—better choices. First, however, there's one last (but not least) clutter-contributing factor you need to know about.

LIVING IN THE LAND OF MORE

If you've lived in America since childhood, you have been socialized to get and go instead of to let go. This socialization process begins early, and becomes so deeply ingrained that most people aren't even aware of how it shapes their behavior. I hadn't realized the extent of it myself until I read the following passage in, oddly enough, *The Grief Recovery Handbook*:

> In all our formative learning, the overwhelming emphasis is placed on learning how to acquire both material and non-material things in order to make life a successful and happy event. In early childhood we try to acquire our parents' praise. Later we try to acquire toys at Christmas or Hannukah by being good. We try to acquire good grades in school in order to gain approval.... This process of learning how to acquire things continues unabated even into our adult lives. Certainly the advertising industry understands this phenomenon when its marketing campaigns focus on finding happiness and contentment through the acquisition of things.
> —*From* The Grief Recovery Handbook *by John W. James and Frank Cherry*

When you are taught that acquiring is good, it follows that *not* acquiring is *not* good. More is better; therefore less is worse. This perception is so central to our culture that people rarely question it. Did you ever see that bumper sticker. "Whoever dies with the most toys, wins"? I think many people never realized that it was supposed to be a joke.

Years ago, I visited Hearst Castle and was struck by the thought that William Randolph Hearst had a major clutter problem. Not only is the castle itself packed with his acquisitions, but he had accumulated warehouses full of stuff! Yet nobody ever refers to these things as "clutter." Why? Because of the widespread perception that wealth confers a sense of respectability on clutter. (The wealthy people who call me to help them with their clutter don't buy that concept—but they do seem to buy everything else.)

Hearst suffered from a condition I call *redundabundance*: the unrestricted desire and ability to obtain more and more of what you already have too much of. In the past, redundabundance was a rich-person's disease, like dyspepsia. What's changed since Hearst's heyday, of course, is that you no longer actually have to have wealth to be a victim of redundabundance. (Credit cards are all you need.) So now it seems most Americans have caught it. Much has already been written about this peculiar syndrome (called *affluenza* by other witty researchers). Therefore, I won't waste your time with lists of boring statistics. Nor will I provide one of those silly quizzes designed to prove the obvious. I figure since you're reading this book, it's quite likely you already recognize you've got redundabundance. What you want is an antidote for it—a "clutter cure."

The next chapter will put you on the path to discovering one.

CHAPTER WRAP-UP

- Letting go of stuff goes against our basic instinct to acquire and hoard.
- Regretting past choices keeps you chained to "clutter ghosts" and provides an excuse to hang on to existing clutter.
- Holding on to something that never worked for you in the first place does not justify the money spent on the object.

- Being socialized to keep getting more stuff creates redundabun-dance: the unrestricted desire and ability to obtain more and more of what you already have too much of.
- If you find yourself grieving over the loss of something that was never alive to begin with, seek counseling.

What Is Clutter?

● ●

A primary step in letting go of clutter is to clarify what it means to you. Why? Because sometimes the emotional baggage attached to clutter is almost as weighty as the clutter itself.

This chapter gets you to focus on exactly what you want to let go of. After all, to hit a target, you first need to know where to aim. Focusing on your clutter target is a two-step process:

 CLARIFYING CLUTTER—Examining different connotations, definitions, and examples of clutter to help you clarify both what it means to you and how it is affecting your life

 CLASSIFYING CLUTTER—Pinpointing the clutter categories and areas that you want to target for decluttering

IS CLUTTER BAD?

Like beauty, clutter is in the eye of the beholder. (Of course, if it's actually getting in your eye, that could be a problem.) "One person's clutter may be another's treasure," to paraphrase an old saying. But the word *clutter* is used interchangeably with trash, litter, mess, disorder. So it would seem that clutter is bad.

Yet there's another side to clutter: a comfy, familiar, welcoming side. It's the opposite of sterile and cold. For example, the phrase "comfortably cluttered" might connote a cozy cottage, a delightful little gift shop, a favorite old bookstore, or perhaps your great-grandmother's treasure-filled attic. Wonderful antique stores are often appealingly cluttered, as are many successful artists' studios, charming gardens, and quirky museums. And Victorian- and Country-style decor are dependent on a certain amount of "collectible clutter." Therefore, clutter doesn't always mean chaos; sometimes it means comfort. So clutter can be good.

The point is, clutter is only as bad—or good—as it makes you feel. Since you're reading this book, it's probably safe to assume that your clutter is not making you feel particularly good. But no matter how you feel about clutter, it's important that you acknowledge this fact: You are not your clutter.

● ●
Unlabel Yourself
Having clutter does not necessarily mean that you are lazy, undisciplined, dirty, or any of the other negative labels you may have consciously or subconsciously attached to yourself because of your own or others' judgments.
● ●

IS CLUTTER DIRTY?

One phrase I never use is "clutter cleaning." It implies that your clutter is dirty. (Perhaps your clutter *is* dirty, but if you get rid of it then you won't have to worry about cleaning it.) I prefer the term *decluttering:* in my opinion it's more accurate as well as less judgmental.

There seems to be some confusion about the differences between four separate yet related activities: cleaning, neatening, organizing, and decluttering. Here's how I clarify them:

- CLEANING is what you do to remove dust and dirt.
- NEATENING is what you do before guests come over.
- ORGANIZING is what you try to do after the guests have left and you go crazy trying to find what you hid away while you were neatening.
- DECLUTTERING is what you do while you're trying to get organized and you realize: the more clutter you get rid of, the less stuff you'll have to organize.

GLOSSARY

Cleaning: Removing dirt via washing, vacuuming, dusting, scrubbing, and any other cleansing processes.

Decluttering: Discarding, removing, or markedly reducing any accumulation of material objects.

Neatening: Straightening, tidying, and/or hiding things away to create the appearance of orderliness.

Organizing: Putting things in a logical order for the purpose of making it easy to locate them.

CLUTTER IS OVERWHELMING

"What is clutter?" I ask in my Letting Go of Clutter workshop, where thousands of people have shared their personal definitions of *clutter.* "After all, one person's clutter may be another person's bibelots, chotchkas, collections, curios, knicknacks, memorabilia, necessities, souvenirs, supplies, trinkets, treasures . . . or just important stuff. So what I want to know is, what does clutter mean to *you?*" Responses have included:

"Too much stuff and not enough room for it!"

"Things I never know what to do with."

"Whatever I can't seem to get rid of but don't really need."

"Everything in my garage—no room for the car!"

"Boxes and boxes of 'Miscellaneous.'"

"Anything I have no place for that seems to gather dust."

"Too many things clogging up my life."

These answers point to a problem that often overshadows the clutter which creates it: overwhelm. Overwhelm is a condition that causes paralysis of the decision-making muscles. Victims of overwhelm have a tendency to spin in circles, repeating something that sounds like "Where do I start?" over and over again. (This symptom is called *clutter mutter.*) Fortunately, the condition is curable if discovered in time.

When you're overwhelmed by clutter, it's extremely difficult to focus and stay focused on the task at hand. Then you're trapped in a downward spiral: as focus diminishes, overwhelm increases—and vice versa.

OVERWHELM: Victims of overwhelm have a tendency to spin in circles.

The greater your sense of overwhelm, the harder it becomes to let go of clutter.

CLARIFYING CLUTTER

Focus requires clarity of purpose. Finding clarity in clutter may seem incongruous, but it's a useful incongruity. Clarifying what clutter means to you can help you (a) focus on what you want to let go of, and then (b) decide where to start. Let's begin the clarification process by defining clutter. If you look in a dictionary, you'll actually find several definitions. The first definition probably comes closest to most people's general concept of clutter: "A crowded or confused mass or collection; litter, disorder." But it's the second definition that I find most compelling: "Interfering echoes visible on a radar screen caused by reflection from objects other than the target."

WHERE WOULD YOU BE WITHOUT YOUR CLUTTER?

Write down what you'd be doing if you weren't allowing clutter to obstruct you:

_____

_____

_____

_____

_____

_____

_____

_____

_____

_____

_____

_____

What this means is that clutter is whatever you perceive as creating interference in your life and distracting you from what you think is more important. As a man in one of my workshops once put it, "Clutter is stuff that gets in my way when I'm trying to do something else."

Clutter is therefore a two-headed beast: What clutter does and what it *is* are equally problematic.

"Clutter is what allows you to procrastinate, to sit on the sidelines while life parades by outside the window," one woman told me. She had been decluttering for a year in anticipation of a cross-country move. In the process she found herself uncovering all sorts of incomplete plans, unfinished projects, and deferred dreams.

What is *your* clutter interfering with or distracting you from?

CLUTTER IS A LUXURY

I have several definitions of clutter myself. In one respect, I think clutter is a luxury. And I can prove to you that it's a luxury you can't really afford. No, wait. I'll let you prove it to yourself, because that's more effective. Take three minutes to fill out the Time = $ Worksheet, on the following page, and you'll see what I mean.

Based on their answers to the Time = $ Worksheet, my workshop participants have reported that the amount of time they've wasted (due to clutter-related causes) has cost them between $500 and $82,000 a year! So now you can understand why I think clutter can be viewed as a luxury. It certainly costs more than it's worth.

But clutter is also more than a luxury. I see it as a stress producer, too. I think clutter can be defined as *anything creating stress for you because of its appearance, condition, location, arrangement, or quantity.*

No matter what you choose to call clutter, one thing seems certain: clutter is whatever you want to let go of, but haven't—yet.

Can You Really Afford Your Clutter?

How your time = $$$

Your wage per hour: $_____

Note: If you are salaried or do not otherwise earn a set dollar amount per hour, estimate what you feel your time is worth based on a 40-hour workweek.

Examples:
  $30,000/yr = $14.42/hr
  $40,000/yr = $19.23/hr
  $50,000/yr = $24.04 hr

How much time do you spend per day:
- Locating papers? _____ (minutes/hours)
- Looking for misplaced items? _____
- Being annoyed because you can't find things? _____
- Duplicating efforts? _____

Total wasted time per day: _____
  × $_____ hourly wage
  = $_____
  × 5 days per week
  = $_____
  × 4 Weeks per month
  = $_____
  × 12 months
  = $_____ wasted per year

● ●

When Clutter Does Not Equal Mess

Clutter isn't always about mess and disorder. It can consist of too much stuff that is carefully arranged. Order may camouflage excess.

● ●

WHAT IS *NOT* CLUTTER?

In one of my workshops, a woman asked plaintively, "Do you think teddy bears are clutter?" I answered, "Not if they make you feel good!"

When it comes to defining what isn't clutter, I think the nineteenth-century designer William Morris said it best: "Have nothing in your houses that you do not know to be useful, or believe to be beautiful."

But keep this in mind too: Even useful and/or beautiful things become clutter when you have too many of them, or if they are kept in a way that diminishes their value to you.

CLASSIFYING CLUTTER

Another key step in letting go of clutter is to categorize what you have. Why? Because it gives you a way to break down your decluttering project into manageable pieces.

"When you think of your clutter, what specifically comes to mind?" This is how I rephrase the original question ("What is clutter?") when my workshop participants provide nonspecific answers. Here are some of their responses:

"Piles and piles of paper."

"Clothes that don't fit anymore but are too nice to get rid of."

"Books, videos, photos I can't bear to part with."

"Old cards and letters, sentimental stuff ..."

"Thousands of little hotel toiletries."

"Endless newspapers and magazines."

"Broken appliances I want to fix but never get around to."

"Stacks of junk mail."

"Kids' toys and games."

The list goes on...and on...and on.

Let's go beyond other people's definitions and answer the question, "What specifically comes to mind when I think of my clutter?" Use the Clutter Checklists on the following pages to help you focus on the specific types and areas of things that are cluttering up your life.

Completing these checklists is a crucial step in your letting-go-of-clutter program. By focusing your mind, they will help you focus your energies as you continue on with the decluttering process.

CHAPTER WRAP-UP

- Clutter is anything creating stress for you because of its appearance, condition, location, arrangement, or quantity.
- Clutter is only as bad—or good—as it makes you feel.
- Clutter is whatever you want to let go of, but haven't—yet.
- What clutter does, and what it is, can be equally problematic.
- The greater your sense of overwhelm, the harder it is to let go of clutter.
- Decluttering is a process separate from cleaning, neatening, or organizing.

CLUTTER CATEGORIES CHECKLIST

Put a double checkmark (√√) next to the items that you think create your worst clutter problems. Put a single checkmark (√) next to the ones that cause a lesser, yet still noticeable, degree of clutter. (I recommend using a pencil or an erasable pen.)

Papers

_____ Addresses and Phone Numbers

_____ Banking (ATM slips, statements, checks, etc.)

_____ Brochures and Fliers

_____ Business Cards

_____ Calendars

_____ Cartoons

_____ Catalogs

_____ Clippings

_____ Coupons

_____ Correspondence

_____ Greeting Cards

_____ Mail (bills, junk mail, etc.)

_____ Magazines

_____ Maps

_____ Newspapers

_____ Notes and Lists

_____ Paid Bills

_____ Receipts

_____ Recipes

_____ School Papers

_____ Other: _____

(Continues)

CLUTTER CATEGORIES CHECKLIST (CONTINUED)

Supplies

_____ Arts and Crafts/Hobbies

_____ Bags

_____ Bath and Kitchen (paper & plastic products)

_____ Boxes

_____ Candles

_____ Cleaning and Laundry

_____ Computer-related

_____ Cooking/Food

_____ Cosmetics and/or Toiletries

_____ Electrical (batteries, bulbs, cords)

_____ Gardening

_____ Gift Wrap/Ribbons

_____ Office

_____ Packing/Shipping

_____ Party/Entertaining

_____ Pet

_____ Other: _____

Household

_____ Appliances and/or Gadgets

_____ Books

_____ CDs and/or Audiotapes and/or LPs

_____ Collections or Knickknacks

_____ Decorations (holiday, etc.)

_____ Dining and Kitchenware (china, glasses, cutlery, food storage containers)

(Continues)

Household *(Continued)*

_____ Errand-related

_____ Furnishings

_____ Greeting Cards/Stationery

_____ Linens/Towels

_____ Memorabilia

_____ Photos/Negatives/Slides

_____ School-related

_____ Sports and/or Exercise Equipment

_____ Tools

_____ Toys and/or Games

_____ Vases and/or Candlesticks

_____ Videos and/or DVDs

_____ Other:

Clothing and Accessories

_____ Apparel (slacks, shirts, suits, dresses)

_____ Belts

_____ Gloves

_____ Hats

_____ Jewelry

_____ Outerwear (coats, jackets)

_____ Purses/Totebags/Briefcases

_____ Scarves/Ties

_____ Shoes

_____ Undergarments

_____ Other: _____

CLUTTER AREAS CHECKLIST

Put a double checkmark (√√) next to the areas that you think contain your worst clutter problems. Put a single checkmark (√) next to the ones that cause a lesser, yet still noticeable, amount of clutter. If there is more than one of a particular area (e.g., bedrooms), list or describe in the blanks provided. (I recommend using a pencil or an erasable pen.)

Example: √√ *Bedroom(s): <u>master bedroom; Mary's room</u>*

_____ Attic

_____ Basement

_____ Bathroom(s): _____

_____ Bedroom(s): _____

_____ Briefcase or Totebag

_____ Car/Vehicle

_____ Children's Room(s): _____

_____ Closet(s): _____

_____ Den

_____ Dining Area

_____ Entertainment Center

_____ Entryway

_____ Garage

_____ Guest Room

_____ Hall

_____ Home Office

_____ Kitchen/Pantry

_____ Livingroom

(Continues)

CLUTTER AREAS CHECKLIST (CONTINUED)

_____ Purse

_____ Storage Area(s)

_____ Workplace (business or job)

_____ Yard(s)

_____ Other: _____

The Present

• •

Dealing with Your
Current Clutter

Banishing Your "Energy Enemies"

● ●

A crucial step in letting go of clutter is to discover effective sources of motivation. Why? Because motivation helps keep you energized; without it, it's almost impossible to get started and keep going.

OVERVIEW

This chapter shows you how to get and stay motivated so you can let go of clutter—now and forever. Motivation gives you the energy to tackle overwhelming decluttering projects; it also gives you the strength to continue even when those projects seem endless. These processes can help fuel the fire of your motivation:

1. GIVING YOURSELF CREDIT

2. FOCUSING AND VISUALIZING

3. USING SOUND EFFECTS

4. REWARDING YOURSELF

5. INVOLVING OTHERS

ENERGY VERSUS MOTIVATION

In the middle of one of my workshops, a young man sitting in the back row spoke up. "My biggest problem is that I don't seem to have the energy to deal with my clutter," he said wearily. "I start to go through a pile and then ..." He rolled his eyes and flopped forward, feigning exhaustion, and I, along with the rest of the class, laughed in recognition and empathy.

I was glad he'd raised that problem. It made me realize I hadn't been addressing what I call the *energy enemies:* those enervating emotions that can disable and derail the decluttering process:

Anxiety

Boredom

Distractedness

Fatigue

Grief

Hopelessness

Overwhelm

Resistance

● ●

Doctor's Orders

If you lack energy overall—not just when contemplating your clutter—maybe you're due for a checkup. There are a host of possibilities that could be at the root of your malaise: anemia, sleep deprivation, and depression are three of the most common causes. If your doctor gives you a clean bill of health, you can probably rest assured that there's nothing wrong with you—except perhaps for a curable condition: *declutter procrastinitis.*

● ●

There are two ruthlessly effective ways in which energy enemies can defeat your plans to let go of clutter: by stopping you before you start and by preventing you from continuing. So what can you do to fight back and overcome these undermining emotions?

One answer: Get motivated. Motivation fuels energy: when you're motivated, you feel empowered, and when you feel empowered, you become energized.

HOW TO GET STARTED AND KEEP GOING

During my many years of professional decluttering, I've discovered several effective processes for maintaining motivation. Some of these processes involve attitude adjustment exercises; others are action-oriented activities. Some may work better for helping you get started, while others can be useful for motivating you to keep going. Different processes work for different people at different times.

Motivation Processes to Help You Let Go of Clutter

1. Giving Yourself Credit

When you keep beating yourself up for your past failures and/or the ones you're anticipating, your energy level takes a beating too.

Combats Hopelessness and Anxiety

• •

Sound Familiar?

"I'm no good at this.... I can't make decisions.... I'll never get through these piles.... What's the use, it's hopeless...." This is the clutter mantra that defeats you before you begin, turning your energy into ennui.

• •

Many of us tend to focus attention on our perceived lacks while dismissing and discounting the things we do well or that come easily to us. You may not even realize you're doing this because it's an insidious pattern, and a common one, too. But the more we do this, the more we sabotage ourselves, and the harder it gets to make efforts toward improvement. (I'm not saying you shouldn't pay any attention to your flaws and foul-ups; I just think your good traits and triumphs deserve at least equal time.)

You can break this demotivation pattern by making a conscious effort to acknowledge what you're already doing well. Start with the simple habits you take for granted. For example, perhaps you're a stickler for paying your bills on time; or maybe you're good about putting away new purchases (groceries, supplies, clothes) as soon as they're brought in; or maybe you never let the laundry pile up.

Such habits may be enviable to you if you don't have them; yet if you do have these habits, to you they're "no big deal" or "nothing." But realize this: these "nothings" are the little things that, when absent, contribute to the cluttering-up of life.

I have a favorite saying:

"Life is 5 percent joy, 5 percent grief, and 90 percent maintenance." Think about it—90 percent of what we do is stuff we need to do over and over and over again. From what I've observed, most people are actually managing their 90 percent pretty well, overall. The problem is, when maintenance is lacking in even a small number of life areas, clutter can creep up on you. (Then it becomes part of the 5 percent grief segment.)

Joy: 5%
Grief: 5%
Maintenance: 90%
Life

I'll bet you're already doing plenty of things right—even if you don't think so. No matter how cluttered, disorganized, or messy you may believe you are, it's likely you have certain habits that actually help you function well in more than one area of your life. When you acknowledge those habits and give yourself credit for them, it gives you a boost and helps motivate you to do better in other areas. You see, if you keep beating yourself over the head with guilt about your cluttering habits, you'll just beat yourself down; but if you give yourself a pat on the back, you can propel yourself forward.

The accompanying Household and Personal Maintenance Checklist has two purposes. It's designed to help you: (a) acknowledge how much of your 90 percent maintenance you're already doing well enough; and (b) identify which specific areas you want to target for improvement.

Tip: If you decide to target any areas for improvement, I recommend scheduling daily, weekly, or seasonal maintenance time for regularly accomplishing the tasks relating to those areas.

HOUSEHOLD AND PERSONAL MAINTENANCE CHECKLIST

Instructions:

1. Put a checkmark (✓) by each task or area that you feel you maintain consistently well enough. Put an "**X**" by each task you'd like to do better and/or more regularly. Ignore any tasks that do not apply to your current living situation.

2. Count up the checkmarks and Xs and total them here.
   ✓: _____ X: _____

(Continues)

3. Acknowledge yourself for whatever tasks you are doing well. (Ideas for rewards can be found later in this chapter.)
4. Schedule regular maintenance time for tasks or areas in which you'd like to see improvement; or see if you can delegate any to others (e.g., family members or service providers).

Bedrooms

_____ Making bed(s)

_____ Changing bedding

_____ Other: _____

Cleaning, General

_____ Cleaning bathroom(s)

_____ Dusting

_____ Vacuuming

_____ Cleaning floors

_____ Washing windows

_____ Other: _____

Decluttering and Organizing

_____ Putting things away

_____ Reorganizing closets, cabinets, drawers, etc.

_____ Purging excess possessions

_____ Weeding files

_____ Adding new files

_____ Other: _____

(Continues)

Errands

_____ Dropping off/picking up dry cleaning

_____ Banking

_____ Hardware store or other frequently visited store(s)

_____ Returning things (library books, video rentals, stuff to stores, etc.)

_____ Other: _____

Home Office/Business

_____ Processing incoming mail

_____ Paying bills

_____ Filing/handling household paperwork

_____ Correspondence (including e-mail)

_____ Money maintenance (e.g., balancing checkbook, budgeting, tracking investments)

_____ Computer (backing up hard drive, deleting old files, etc.)

_____ Reading

_____ Planning/time management

_____ Other: _____

Kitchen

_____ Meal planning

_____ Grocery shopping

_____ Putting away groceries

_____ Cooking

_____ Setting and clearing table

_____ Washing dishes/loading dishwasher

_____ Drying dishes/unloading dishwasher

(Continues)

Kitchen *(Continued)*

_____ Putting away dishes

_____ Cleaning

_____ Other: _____

Laundry/Mending

_____ Gathering and sorting laundry

_____ Loading washing machine/dryer

_____ Folding clean laundry

_____ Ironing/steaming

_____ Putting away clean laundry

_____ Sewing buttons, repairing seams, patching holes, etc.

_____ Other: _____

Outside/Landscape

_____ Mowing lawn

_____ Weeding

_____ Watering/fertilizing

_____ Other: _____

Pets

_____ Feeding pets

_____ Washing/grooming pet(s)

_____ Walking dog

_____ Cleaning up after dog

_____ Emptying litterbox, cleaning aquarium/cages, etc.

_____ Veterinary visits

_____ Other: _____

(Continues)

Seasonal

_____ Shopping for gifts

_____ Writing thank-yous

_____ Wrapping gifts

_____ Entertaining (planning and follow-through)

_____ Putting up decorations

_____ Taking down decorations

_____ Other: _____

Trash/Recycling

_____ Gathering trash inside house to put in outside containers

_____ Putting out trash containers for pick up

_____ Putting recycling at curb (if you have this service)

_____ Taking recycling to recycling center

_____ Other: _____

Vehicle(s)

_____ Checking/replacing tires

_____ Taking cars for tune-ups

_____ Checking/replacing fluids

_____ Washing/waxing

_____ Clearing out trunk, glove box, seats, etc.

_____ Other: _____

Any Other Types of Maintenance Not Listed Here

_____

_____

(Continues)

HOUSEHOLD AND PERSONAL MAINTENANCE CHECKLIST (CONTINUED)

Any Other Types of Maintenance Not Listed Here

_____

_____

_____

_____

2. Focusing and Visualizing

Combats Distractedness and Overwhelm

When you feel overwhelmed by the scope of your clutter, it can be very difficult to decide where to start. Just contemplating a pile of stuff, not to mention a houseful, may cause you to fall into a stupor of indecision. As your clutter-clouded gaze shifts from one place (or pile) to another, your attention ping-pongs back and forth. Meanwhile, time, energy, and good intentions drain away.

You can overcome overwhelm by breaking your decluttering project into segments and visualizing desirable results. This process works to give you a sense of focus, and focus feeds motivation. Try these three focusing steps.

STEP ONE: Right now, if it is convenient for you to do so, take "before" pictures of your clutter. (Note: If you haven't got a working camera or cannot easily locate one, it's OK to skip this step for now. I don't want you using it as a delaying tactic and then blaming me.) Do at least one shot of each "clutter clump" or area of concern. By the way, if you don't get around to developing these photos for a while, that's all right. The act of looking through a camera lens is what helps you focus now. The photos themselves will be more motivating later, after you've made visible progress.

THE IMPORTANCE OF VISUALIZING DESIRABLE OUTCOMES

It's motivating to see what you're working toward. That's why we love to look at "before and after" photos; they give us a sense of what's possible. But how do you create your own "after" picture while you're still deep in the throes of "before"? How can you conjure up an oasis of order while staring at a major mess? Try this:

- On a blank sheet of paper, sketch out how you would like the room to look once it has been decluttered and rearranged. Sketch as simply or as elaborately as you wish; don't let any perceived lack of artistic ability hold you back.

- If you are a collage-maker and have saved images you'd like to use with your sketch, by all means do so—unless it would take you longer to find the clippings than it would to make the collage. (Memo to creative procrastinators: Just *do* the exercise. It doesn't have to be done perfectly; remember, you won't be graded on this.)

- Imagine how you will feel once you've let go of whatever is currently cluttering up that room or space. Close your eyes and picture yourself doing something enjoyable and/or productive there. (Note: Doing nothing does qualify as doing something enjoyable.) Let yourself savor how good it feels to be in a space that you have rescued from clutter's clutches.

VISUALIZE DESIRABLE OUTCOMES: Imagine how you'll feel once you've let go of whatever is cluttering up your space.

● ●

FROM VISUALIZING TO VISIBLE-IZING

Motivate yourself by creating noticeable results quickly: Begin by de-cluttering the easiest and most visible clutter area or segment.

● ●

STEP TWO: Review your completed checklists (Clutter Categories and Clutter Areas) from Chapter Two. Because looking through your camera lens in Step One may have caused you to reevaluate some of your responses, you might want to add or subtract checkmarks (I hope you used pencil!). Then list your top clutter priorities below. By "priorities" I mean the things that bother you most.

Decluttering Priorities (*Items/Areas*)

1. _____
2. _____
3. _____

STEP THREE: Now you're ready to create your Focus Plan. The Focus Plan form on the following pages will help you focus on why you want to let go of clutter, what benefits you'll gain from doing so, how you will go about it, and when you plan to finish the project. It's not an easy form to complete, but once you do, you'll be more motivated than ever to get going on let go-ing.

3. Using Sound Effects

Deciding where to begin is important, yet it's only part of the clutter conundrum. Being motivated to get going but not knowing when and how to start can be like having your engine race while it's stuck in neutral.

Combats Boredom and Distractedness

Imagine the beginning of a race: the Indy 500, say, or any kind of sporting race. Horse races, Olympic events, pie-eating contests…What do they all have in common? An official, highly audible starting ritual—a pistol shot, a trumpet call, or some other kind of unmistakable "*go*" sound.

In your race to let go of clutter, a starting ritual can motivate you to get going and keep going. One tool that's useful for this purpose is an old-fashioned dial timer, or kitchen timer. The simple act of turning the dial arrow (and producing that distinctive "sc-c-ritchzz" sound) is an announcement of your commitment to begin.

But that's only the first of several ways in which using a timer can help you during your decluttering sessions. Setting a ticking timer for 15-

FOCUS PLAN

The purpose of this form is to help you focus on *why* you wish to undertake a project; *what* you hope to achieve upon its completion; *how* you plan to accomplish it successfully; *when* you'd like to see it finished; to *whom* you can delegate aspects of it (or the entire project); and *costs* involved. Be as specific as possible.

Project Description/Working Title: _____

_____

Purpose (Why): _____

_____

_____

Goal (What): _____

_____

_____

Plan (How): _____

_____

_____

_____

_____

(Continues)

FOCUS PLAN (CONTINUED)

Deadline/Timeline (When): _____

_____

Delegation (Who): _____

_____

_____

Costs Involved (Products or Services): _____

_____

_____

_____

_____

Benefit(s)/Reward(s) and/or Negative Incentives: _____

_____

_____

_____

_____

_____

minute increments also is a good tactic for keeping you on track instead of sidetracked. The tick-tick-tick serves as an audible, ongoing reminder that time is marching on and not standing still for you while you putter with your clutter. It can prevent you from dawdling over old newspaper clippings or even older love letters—two common triggers of a condition I call *Sidetracking Syndrome.*

CREATE A DECLUTTERING DEADLINE

Sometimes you need more than a 15-minute warning bell to make you keep moving forward. A real deadline, the kind that involves accountability, may be the answer. Here are some effective deadline-setting gambits:

- Invite houseguests.
- Send out party invitations.
- Advertise a yard sale.
- Make an appointment with a service person such as a house-cleaner, repair person, cable installer, etc. (Note: If you have a habit of cancelling appointments, skip this option or make appointments only with people who charge cancellation fees, so you'll be more likely to keep your commitment.)
- Plan to move. (Admittedly a last resort.)

A timer is also useful for reminding you when to move your focus to another area or when to stop so you'll be on time for an appointment. It's hard to ignore that loud, insistent *bzzz-zzz-t* which announces "time's up!" in a universally recognizable way. Also, setting a short-term goal along with a timer (e.g., 15 minutes to clear out a drawer) can give you a sort of "beat the clock" rush, which helps banish boredom.

Tip: Go back to the Decluttering Priorities list you made earlier in the chapter and pencil in a time estimate next to each one. If your timer buzzes before a goal is achieved, make a quick guess as to the amount of additional time needed to finish. Then reset it—and keep going!

● ●

Do the Declutter Dance

Music is another sound-effective motivating tool. The right beat can get you moving—and it can get your clutter moving, too, once you click into your "tossing rhythm." Any type of music that lifts your spirits and quickens your pace works well as a decluttering aid. Aerobics tapes, marching music, rock, rap, opera, bagpipes, Beethoven—whatever wakes you up and shakes you up.

● ●

4. Rewarding Yourself

When you have no real incentive to let go of clutter, it's hard to get started and keep going. This is especially true if you feel that "a job well done is its own reward," as the old saying goes. A decluttering job that looks like a lifetime project, with no glimmer of light at the end of the tunnel, can look pretty unrewarding.

You can create your own light at the end of the tunnel by promising yourself a gift that gives you an incentive to move forward—something that brightens your outlook (a lamp, perhaps). Incentives can be powerful motivators. Here's a three-step process for creating your very own "Let Go of Clutter Incentive Program."

First, redefine the word *Done*. Challenge your assumption that a job is "done" only when every part of it is completed. The purpose of some of those checklists and forms you've been filling out is to help you break down your clutter into manageable pieces. Depending on how massive or minor your decluttering project is, you may or may not need to segment it further. For example, if you have a large home or office space with many densely cluttered rooms, it might be helpful to approach each room segment by segment (e.g., closet, drawers, floor, etc.).

Of course, ideally you'd be able to get all the segments in all the rooms decluttered in just one session, and then it would be "done." (By all means, dream.) But assuming you are a busy, Earth-based life form, completing one or more segments per session is probably more realistic. So let yourself redefine *done* to mean "finished ____ part(s)" (you fill in the blank).

Next, set mini-goals.   Before you get started, decide which segment(s) you want to have completed by the end of the session. Jot down a quick list of up to three mini-goals with a target time for each one. For example:

1. Top desk drawer—15 minutes
2. Under desk—20 minutes
3. Desk top—30 minutes

You don't need a special form for this; go ahead and use a piece of that scratch paper you've been hoarding.

Finally, choose your rewards.   Now you get to think about how you'd like to celebrate your successes each time you manage to accomplish your mini-goals. It's motivating to have rewards in mind; they can help you acknowledge the sense of accomplishment you might otherwise deny yourself.

● ●
Bribing Your Inner Child
When it comes to letting go of stuff, sometimes your Inner Child speaks up quite assertively: "You can't make me!" If this happens,

remember that bribing the Inner Child may be your best option. It's a lot easier than arguing with the little beast.

● ●

Rewards don't have to cost any money or take much time. Use the Rewards form on the following pages to help you think of incentives to motivate your decluttering process.

● ●

Outgrowing Past Choices

If you find yourself resisting the letting-go process, stop for a moment and take stock of your feelings. Are you uncomfortable, defensive, or angry? These feelings fuel resistance, a common energy enemy. Sit quietly for five minutes and let yourself think about why you're feeling like this. Perhaps on a subconscious level you sense you are being made wrong in some way. But letting go of past choices doesn't necessarily mean that you made bad or stupid choices or that you were wrong for having chosen them. It just means that you have outgrown them and are now ready to move on. Accept that choosing to let go of something now is not an invalidation of your original impulse.

● ●

REWARDS

"Virtue is its own reward." Perhaps—but sometimes we need other forms of motivation! Plan to treat yourself to something special each time you manage to complete something you've previously procrastinated on doing or when you finish part (or all) of a project.

(Continues)

Below are some rewards categories, with spaces for you to fill in specific kinds of rewards that appeal to you. The rewards should be appropriate to your budget and realistic in terms of your lifestyle and available time.

Places to Go

Ideas: Art Galleries, Scenic Drive, Bookstores, Museums, Parks, Window Shopping

_____

_____

_____

_____

Arts/Entertainment

Ideas: Comedy, Concerts, Dance, Movies, Theatre, Video

_____

_____

_____

_____

To Read/Hear

Ideas: Books, CDs/Tapes/Albums, Lectures/Classes, Magazines

_____

_____

_____

(Continues)

Gifts

Ideas: Flowers, Cookies, Wine

_____

_____

_____

Romance

Ideas: Candlelight Dinner, Bubblebath, Hot Tub, Massage

_____

_____

_____

Miscellaneous

You name it:

_____

_____

_____

5. Involving Others

If you're a "people person" who enjoys being around others and dislikes spending much time alone, the prospect of decluttering all by yourself—just you and your piles—may cause you to

Combats Fatigue and Grief

feel fatigued and listless before you even get started. Or perhaps you're not super-sociable, but you need to make commitments with others in order to get things done; for example, some people are only able to maintain an exercise regimen because they have a "fitness buddy" to work out with.

So why not have a "clutter buddy"? If you have any friends who have complained about their own clutter, see if they'd be interested in teaming up with you for clutter-buddy duty. If you don't know anyone with whom you'd feel comfortable decluttering, it may be time to look into hiring someone to help you. (See Appendix B for resources.)

A MATTER OF LIFE AND DEATH

It's true that decluttering can be a daunting, dismaying, and discouraging process even under the best of circumstances. But under the worst of circumstances—the death of a loved one—it often seems like an impossible job, one that's far too painful to tackle alone.

Both grief and fatigue are energy enemies that tend to be impervious to most motivation processes. Sometimes these emotions exist in tandem, or together with any or all of the other energy enemies. Being faced with the task of going through the belongings of a deceased loved one while you are still grieving is one of the most difficult experiences. I have found that the best way to get through it successfully is to have help, preferably from people who are not as grief-stricken as you. Sometimes friends or even other family members can be called upon for assistance, but if it all possible see if you can hire a neutral party such as an organizer or an estate liquidator. (*Note:* Realtors are often a good source of contacts for finding this type of help.)

The same advice applies if you are truly experiencing fatigue or if you suffer from a disability or condition that makes it difficult (or impossible) to declutter on your own. Involving others is crucial. (See Appendix B for information on finding assistance.)

MOTIVATED BY PAIN

The motivation methods described in this chapter have already helped many people let go of clutter. I hope you are helped, too. But there's one more motivation source that only you can provide for yourself. And it may be the most effective one of all. It's called pain. Now, don't get the wrong idea—I'm not talking about the S&M variety here. The pain I'm referring to is emotional pain.

I came upon a quote one day that explains why certain people who say they really want to let go of clutter just don't do it.

> "I believe pain is an essential motivating tool in the quest to better one's life...no one moves who's not in enough pain." —*Kenny Loggins (quoted in* Quiet Triumphs)

Ultimately, if something pains you enough, you will do what needs to be done to change it. But if it doesn't bother you enough—if you can live with things the way they are—you may not be ready to change anything.

If you've been saying, "I hate having all this clutter, but I just can't seem to get rid of it," you're giving yourself a mixed message. This contributes to making you feel clutter-crazed. I think it's much healthier to admit, "Well, I'd really like it if my life was uncluttered, but I hate decluttering. Therefore, I'm not going to do it. I'll just live with things the way they are, and I'm not going to feel bad about it."

So stop giving yourself contradictory messages, and either get going on let go-ing or choose to feel OK about staying cluttered. It all comes down to your making a choice. You have a right to keep all your clutter, but you also have to live with the outcome of keeping it. If you don't like the results, change the choice. And if you're not ready to change the choice, you're probably not in enough pain!

● ●

Lose the Wait

The good thing about clutter is that it will wait for you. The bad thing about clutter is that it will wait for you. It will just wait and wait for you until it bothers you enough to do something about it.

● ●

CHAPTER WRAP-UP

- If you feel like you just don't have enough energy to deal with your clutter, yet there's nothing medically wrong with you, a lack of motivation may be the real problem.
- Energy-draining emotions can be counteracted by using a variety of motivation processes.
- Life is 5 percent joy, 5 percent grief, and 90 percent maintenance—give yourself the credit you deserve for managing so much of that 90 percent.
- Breaking down your decluttering projects into segments makes them seem less overwhelming.
- A ticking timer and the right music can help motivate you to get started and keep going.
- Recognize when you need other people to help you.
- If you just can't seem to be sufficiently motivated to let go of clutter, perhaps it's not creating enough pain for you.

Purging Paper and Preventing Piles

● ●

An important step in letting go of clutter is learning how to exorcise your excess papers. Why? Because pound for pound, paper clutter is often more complex and difficult to deal with than non-paper clutter, creating stress as well as mess.

OVERVIEW

This chapter provides you with techniques and tips for conquering paper clutter of all kinds. Because we are living in a time of incessantly flowing, infinite information, we need special systems and processes to help us both purge paper and prevent it from piling up. These systems and processes include:

1. THE THREE-SYSTEM PILE PREVENTION PROGRAM

2. THE THREE-SPEED PURGING PROCESS

Most of the people who attend my workshops and/or hire me to work with them have this in common: they suffer from a chronic condition I call *Paperosis misplacea.* This is a disorder (pardon the pun) that causes piles of paper to form on, or within, any available surfaces. One of my - Paperosis-infected clients even had a massive pile perched atop her paper shredder. "That's where I put papers I think I might want to shred someday," she told me earnestly.

CONDENSED CLUTTER

If you take a look at the Clutter Categories Checklist in Chapter Two, you'll see that Paper is only one out of four categories (25 percent). Yet of the Top 10 Clutter Questions, five (50 percent) relate to paper: mail, tax papers, newspaper clippings and magazines, desk-top papers, and paper memorabilia (old cards and letters). No wonder so many people say they feel "buried in paper."

Not only do papers cause a disproportionate amount of mess, they in turn cause a disproportionate amount of stress. Why? Because papers often congeal into what I call *condensed clutter.* Example: One medium-size pile of paper—say, up to a foot high—can contain over a thousand individual pieces of paper. When you compare this to a similar-size pile of non-paper clutter, which might consist of around 10 items (e.g., clothes, toys, videotapes), it's easy to see why paper seems so overwhelming.

● ●
Pointless versus Purposeful Piles
Having piles of paper isn't necessarily bad. It all depends on whether they're a hindrance or a help to you. If the piles are serving a positive purpose (keeping your desk warm in winter?) and you know exactly where to find whatever's in them, then they may not be a problem. But if they're actually pointless piles of procrastination... keep reading.
● ●

Consider this: if you spend an average of just four seconds per piece looking at each paper in a one-foot-high pile, it would probably take you at least one hour to get through the stack. (And I'll bet you're used to spending quite a bit more than four seconds per page.) In the same amount of time, you could probably go through several piles of non-paper clutter. It all comes down to density (of your piles, not your mind). Dense piles just take longer to "de-pile," which means that it can take a long, long time to see results. And that's a key reason why paper clutter is so daunting to deal with.

THE FIVE TYPES OF PILES

As we continue to be bombarded with an infinity of information, the piles get denser, larger, and more prolific. Piles of paper seem to breed faster than fruit flies. According to my many years of research, there are actually five types of pointless piles:

1. **THE GROWING PILE.** It keeps growing bigger and bigger, especially when fed a steady diet of unopened mail, catalogs, and reading materials that never get read.
2. **THE STAGNATING PILE.** This starts out as a Growing Pile, but its growth becomes stunted after it is hastily shoved into a bag, box, drawer, closet, or cabinet (usually after a panic-stricken cry goes up: "someone is coming over!").
3. **THE DIMINISHING PILE.** This is the pile that shows progress: it gets smaller and smaller because you're actually dealing with it instead of adding to it or hiding it away. Unfortunately, this pile invariably becomes . . .
4. **THE DISTILLED PILE.** This pile has gone through the previous stages only to grind to a halt when its contents have been sifted down to sediment, which is composed of "pile germs"— those last few hard pieces of paper that seem impervious to the

Growing   Stagnating Diminishing Distilled Double-Distilled

The Five Types of Piles

decision-making process. These are the papers that get shuffled and reshuffled endlessly because you feel you "just can't decide" what to do with them, and you're never ready to just throw them out. Pile germs lie dormant until they reach the Distilled Pile stage, whereupon they begin to breed. (*Important note:* Pile germs must be killed to stop a pile from breeding. For emergency pile-germ-killing tactics, see The Five Ws of Clutter Control later in this chapter.)

5. THE DOUBLE-DISTILLED PILE. This pile is formed when there are several small, dormant Distilled Piles lying around and, in an effort to "clean up," you combine them, thereby creating one monstrous pile that seems completely impenetrable, because you've already touched the contents hundreds of times and have just about given up on ever figuring out what to do with them.

INFORMATION ANXIETY

The pile phenomenon might not exist except for a modern ailment known as *Information Anxiety*. This condition manifests as an unrealistic desire to keep up with the massive doses of information we're all incessantly bombarded with nowadays. The anxiety is caused by a refusal to accept that the desire is unrealistic. Why is it unrealistic? Because although technology has evolved, the human mind has not. We are living in an age where we have access to more information faster than ever before (and getting ever faster), but we can't process it any more quickly than our primitive ancestors could have.

It doesn't really matter where or how you house your "pointless piles." Whether they're highly visible (desktop-dwelling) or hidden away (drawer-dwelling), horizontally heaped or even vertically filed…all that matters is how you feel about them. If, for example, you are experiencing episodes of pile paranoia ("my piles are out to get me!"), it's time to take action.

Conquering pointless piles and curing Paperosis involve two separate but interrelated processes: prevention and purging.

PREVENTING PAPEROSIS

Two main factors that contribute to Paperosis are fear and ignorance. People are afraid to throw out papers because they don't know what to keep and what can be safely gotten rid of. Fear of regret (covered earlier) is bad enough; fear of the IRS can be worse.

In my workshops, three particular paper-related "fear and ignorance" questions have popped up dozens of times. Here they are, along with the answers:

1. Which Papers Do I Have to Keep?

There are two main types of paper documents: records and resources. Records are finite in quantity (even though sometimes that might seem hard to believe), while resources are infinite (thanks to our technology-powered Information Age). Therefore, the old rule "when in doubt, throw it out" applies mainly to resource materials. You can safely dump stuff like magazine articles and seminar handouts. But when it comes to financial and legal documents, the opposite rule applies: when in doubt, don't throw it out. To eliminate doubt so you can eliminate more paper, get guidelines from your tax adviser or legal counsel. (See the appendixes for guidelines and other sources.)

2. How Long Must I Keep My Records?

Different rules apply to different papers and situations. Some records should be kept indefinitely, others can be discarded after specific periods of time (e.g., seven years), and still others needn't be kept at all. Again, there are general record-keeping guidelines available through tax advisers, the IRS, and other sources provided in Appendix B. As for resource-type papers, it's unlikely the IRS will ever be interested in seeing stuff like your collection of recipes or old travel brochures, so you can safely toss them out whenever you want to. (Soon, I hope.)

Tip: Always make sure the date and source are clearly marked on any resources you choose to save. Undated resources often become useless sources of outdated misinformation.

3. Where and How Should I Keep My Papers?

Certain systems will help you keep your papers under control by preventing Paperosis. The three-system pile prevention program explained in the next section includes:

- a time management system, for scheduling paper maintenance time;
- a paper-flow system, for managing action papers; and
- a filing system, for storing paper records and resources.

THE TWO TYPES OF TIME

If you think that conquering paper clutter takes time, you're only half right. The decluttering process actually requires two types of time: Project time and maintenance time. *Project time* is what you spend to get out from under your existing accumulations. *Maintenance time* is the time you need to invest on a daily or weekly basis to maintain your clutter-free state.

Maintenance time is a concept that many people resist. There's a childlike belief that once a closet is cleared out or a desktop is de-cluttered, it will magically stay that way. Of course it won't, any more than a garden will stay weeded or laundry will stay washed. (But you can always hope.)

Neglecting maintenance time actually creates the need for more project time, because when things aren't maintained, they often cease to function and/or become an unsightly mess. That's why your clutter may actually represent a visible manifestation of uninvested maintenance time.

So, which do you prefer: spending a few minutes a day dealing with incoming clutter, or days of hours burrowing through your backlog?

Perhaps at this point, you need to do both. That's why this chapter provides techniques and tips to help you use your decluttering project time and maintenance time effectively.

Just remember—the more stuff you choose to let go of, the less time you need to spend maintaining it.

THE THREE-SYSTEM PILE PREVENTION PROGRAM

Time Management System

An effective time management system helps prevent piles by allowing you to schedule blocks of time for appointments not only with others but also with yourself. This enables you to establish regular maintenance-time sessions and to break down overwhelming projects into "do-able" segments.

Another way a good time management system works to cure paper-osis is by giving you a place to corral all your little reminder notes. There's nothing actually wrong with making notes on Post-its or bits of paper; the problems occur from what you do—or don't do—with the notes once you've scribbled them. Having a central "home" where you can jot things down, and also transfer notes made elsewhere, helps keep those annoying little scraps under control.

Time management systems, a.k.a. planners or organizers, come in many different styles, sizes, formats, and flavors. (Well, maybe not flavors—yet.) The paper-based kinds are available in a variety of sizes, colors, and materials (e.g., leather-covered binders and spiral-bound notebooks), and the variations of electronic organizers are constantly evolving. These products run the gamut from strikingly simple to confusingly complex.

How do you decide which type of time management system is best for you? Ironically, it takes time because it's a trial-and-error process. Experimenting with different options is really your best bet. (*Note: Organized to Be Your Best!* by Susan Silver has a detailed overview of the best time management products. See Appendix B.)

CONQUERING CALENDAR CLUTTER

One of the simplest time management aids is a desk-blotter-size ruled calendar located on the wall near the phone you use most often. A super-large calendar can provide a good place for notes and lists to come home to roost; it gives you enough room for everything, and the lines make it easier to keep your scribbles in order. Attach a pencil with a string—or a thick chain, if necessary.

Paper-Flow System

Setting up and maintaining an effective paper-flow system is really one of the best ways to keep your desktop clear.

A good paper-flow system gives you an easily accessible, categorized "home" for any papers you need to take action on (e.g., bills to pay, correspondence to answer, documents to file, things to read). This way, when you sit down to do paper maintenance or projects, you don't end up spending half your time looking for what you need. (Winnie-the-Pooh's definition of organizing comes to mind: "Organizing is what you do before you do it so that when you do it, it's not all mixed up.")

There are a variety of options for creating a paper-flow system. Horizontal possibilities include stacking trays, bins, baskets, or multi-slot sorters: one slot or tray is designated for each category of paper, and labeled clearly with the category name. Vertical variations include upright sorters, wall-mounted or magnetic "hot pockets," step-racks, or desktop file-holders, to hold files labeled with the paper categories. (Although many people aren't comfortable with the idea of using files for action papers, it's still an option.)

It really doesn't matter whether you use a horizontal or vertical paper-flow system. My criteria for any effective system are that it must be simple, flexible, and growth-oriented. Whatever you can use comfortably and consistently is a good system for you. But whichever type of paper-flow system you choose needs to have a limited number of broad categories (four to eight is typical), legibly labeled. Common category names include:

To Pay (bills, charitable solicitations)

To Read

To File

Correspondence

Pending/Follow-ups

Events/Invitations

Active Projects/To Do's

To Share/Forward

Note: "In" and "Out" tend to be *too* broad for many people. That's why the "In box" has become a euphemism for "teetering pile of paper."

Before you set up your paper-flow system, you need to accept this truth: the system will not *do* the papers for you! So if you just keep stuffing papers in it without ever removing any, you'll end up with a clogged, overloaded, ineffective system. This is why it's important to pencil appointments into your time management system for regular (daily and/or weekly) paper maintenance time. (Remember the "90 percent maintenance" equation?)

Of course, the more papers you resist acquiring, the less time and space are needed to maintain them.

DON'T "DO OR DIE"

I've noticed it's usually futile to designate a tray as "Urgent," "Hot," "Do or Die," or a similarly frantic-sounding label. Generally speaking, truly urgent paperwork will end up on your chair or heaped in the middle of your desk or dining room table (possibly on top of an older pile). This is reality.

Other common mistakes that sabotage paper-flow systems include:

- Too many categories *or* too few categories
- Labels that aren't readable
- Containers that are too small *or* too large

Filing System

An effective filing system has two functions:

- It helps you locate papers quickly.
- It provides a good home for your papers.

The latter function is particularly helpful for both preventing and purging piles. When you have just the right place to put the papers you want or need to keep, it's easy to put them there. And when something is easy to do, it's likelier to get done.

In general, there are only two types of paper to file, as mentioned earlier: (1) records—what you have to keep and (2) resources—what you *want* to keep. I'm talking about what belongs in an active filing system. Old records (e.g., tax records from previous years) can be archived in file boxes. Sentimental papers (love letters, programs from memorable concerts, etc.) belong elsewhere too, perhaps in a "memories box" (see Chapter Six).

Whether you need to set up a new filing system from scratch (or scraps, as the case may be) or reorganize an existing one, the same process applies: Start out by making a list of file names. If you only have a "piling system" so far, the File Index Sample provided on the next page should give you some ideas to work with. Use the accompanying File Index Form to create your own customized filing system outline.

WHY WAIT TO WEED?

In most cases, I recommend waiting to weed files until after the filing system has been reorganized. I've found that if you try to weed first, you'll find papers that aren't in the right files because the right files don't exist yet. Then you end up making mini-piles with them. But if you reorganize the system first and then weed it, you're more likely to have a place for everything.

FILE INDEX SAMPLE

Financial	Household	Personal	General
Banking • Acct 1 • Acct 2 • Acct 3	Cars/Vehicles	Correspondence	Beauty/Fitness
Bills Paid (12 Months)	Decorating Ideas	Family	Emergency
Budget	Gardening Tips	Friends	Entertainment
Credit Cards (contracts/ receipts)	Household Hints (Cleaning/ organizing)	Gift Ideas (wish lists)	Health Information
Insurance • Auto • Health • Property	Improvements	Lists/ Checklists	Humor (Smile File)
Investments	Instructions/ Warranties	Mate 1 (by name)	Inspiration
Mortgage	Inventory	Mate 2 (by name)	Recipes
Receipts	Repair/ Maintenance Records (gardeners/ handymen, etc.)	Medical Records	Resources (misc.)
Taxes (current year to pre- vious year)		Resumes/ Career Info.	Restaurants
			Travel

Notes:
- The bulleted file names indicate interior folders that go inside the hanging files.
- Notice that file names are in alphabetical order within categories.
- Keep in mind that these are just examples of file names and categories; you may need additional and/or different ones for your own system.

FILE INDEX FORM

This form is for creating your own customized filing system outline. Be sure to use a pencil or erasable pen for flexibility.

There are two main steps in creating or reorganizing a filing system: planning and doing. During the planning stage, you create an outline on paper based on the list you compile. Depending on how many files you anticipate needing, you'll be able to structure your list into either a very simple alphabetized system (if you only need about 20 files or so) or an easy-to-use categorized system. (*Note:* I rarely advocate setting up a numerical or coded filing system except for certain types of industries, e.g., libraries and hospitals. Labels on files used in households and small businesses should be instantly identifiable, so you can find what you need without having to decode it first.)

WHY PLAN?

I've created or reorganized almost 300 filing systems. So please believe me when I tell you that the most important step in the process is planning, which involves creating an outline.

Many people resist this step. They want to jump right in and start moving files around, because this produces the impression that you're actually doing something. You are: you're making a bigger mess. It's like running in circles: Even though you appear to be moving, you're not really getting anywhere.

Here's a way to understand why outlining your system is such a crucial first step. Imagine you're going to build a house. Do you go out and buy the building materials, dump them on the site, and then start digging and drilling? Probably not. Yet many people do the equivalent of this when they set out to create or overhaul a filing system: They buy a whole bunch of folders and maybe even a new file cabinet, and then start digging around in their files and papers until they get discouraged and give up.

So what's a better way? A set of plans—a blueprint—is prepared before any actual house-building project begins. The same process applies when you're building or reorganizing a filing system: draw up your plans first. Making a list of your file names is the first stage of planning. This list will make the reorganizing process much simpler: It lets you see all your file names at a glance, which is much easier than having to open drawer after drawer (or box after box) stuffed with folders. It also helps you spot and eliminate redundancies and inaccuracies.

● ●

Why Make a File Index?

A file index:

- Helps you see all your files at a glance.
- Works as a memory jogger for anyone who has trouble remembering file names and/or categories.
- Saves time when training others to use the system.

● ●

CATEGORIZING VERSUS ALPHABETIZING

Depending on how your mind works, a categorized system (one that's alphabetized within categories) can be much easier to use than an alphabetized uncategorized one. Think about how supermarkets and department stores are set up: products are categorized together based on similarity. Now think about how long it would take you to shop if they were alphabetized instead! Grouping "like items" together is a basic principle of organization as well as a human trait. After all, babies can categorize by color and shape long before they're ready to learn the alphabet.

Once you have your list in hand, look it over and decide whether a straight A-to-Z system will suffice or whether it might be more helpful to group related files alphabetically under broad categories such as Financial, Household, and Personal. The File Index Sample on page 66 provides an outline of some typical file groupings to give you an idea of how a categorized system can work.

If you decide to categorize, go down your list of files and put a potential category name next to each one. Then re-sort your list so files in each category are grouped together. (*Note:* Although it's not essential to use a computer for this, it can really save time and effort in the long run, especially for sorting, alphabetizing, updating, and even making labels.)

Congratulations—your filing system outline, or file index, is now ready for implementation.

IMPLEMENTING YOUR FILING SYSTEM

You've finished planning; now you're ready for the "doing" step. Using your outline, set up your new files. You can make your labels by hand (legibly block printing) or by computer, typewriter, or labeler. Then you'll be ready to transfer or file the contents of the old files—or piles, if that's what you have.

● ●
Smile File
If you're in the habit of clipping cartoons, humorous writing, and/or saving printouts of e-mail joke lists, you might as well give them a good home. Why not set up a "Smile File"? (Unless, of course, you find it funnier to just have piles of these types of papers.) Just be sure to go through the file periodically. You can laugh as you toss.
● ●

FAR-FLUNG FILES

You don't have to house your filing system in a file cabinet, nor do you even need to keep all your files in one place. Consider these options:

File Cart.   An alternative or supplement to the common file cabinet is the rolling file cart, which can fit under a table or counter and can be relocated easily. I often recommend the kind that has an open top, so the files are more accessible. (The ones with lids tend to be "pile magnets", because many people end up leaving papers either on the lid when it's closed, or in the lid when it's open.) However, if you have small children or pets that like to climb, a lidded cart may be a wiser choice.

Fire-Resistant File Safe.   A good place to keep important documents—e.g., birth certificates, passports, licenses, wills, insurance policies—is a fire-resistant file safe. (Sentry makes a decent one which sells for around $50.) In the long run, it's often better than renting a safe deposit box—definitely less expensive and more accessible.

Kitchen Minifile.   If your kitchen is continually plagued with paper piles, consider putting a small file holder on the counter near the phone. (It's a good idea to locate a wastebasket near there as well.) Because kitchens are usually the household hub, it's natural for certain papers to migrate there, especially stuff like coupons, recipes, takeout menus, instructions for kitchen appliances, articles on entertaining and stain removal, and emergency info. Having a kitchen minifile can cut clutter and also save you time on a daily basis in the following ways.

- The papers you want there will always be close at hand so you don't have to go to another room for them.

- Putting those papers back where they belong will be much easier.
- It will help keep kitchen drawers as well as counters free of paper clutter.

Tip: If you like things color-coordinated, you can probably get files to match your kitchen color scheme.

WHAT NOT TO PUT IN YOUR SAFE DEPOSIT BOX

A safe deposit box can be a little too safe for certain documents. Why? Because upon the death of a box holder, a box may be sealed until it is opened by a court order which can be months later. In the meantime, survivors may not have access to the contents. That's why these five types of paper should not be kept in a safe deposit box:

- Cash and/or savings passbooks
- Cemetery deeds
- Insurance policies
- Marriage certificates
- Wills

A fire-resistant file safe may be a better place to store these and other valuable documents such as:

- Birth certificates
- Military discharge records
- Passports
- Property deeds
- Lists of important numbers (bank accounts, credit cards, and phone/address lists)
- Trusts
- Vehicle owner documentation

FORMULA FOR FUNCTIONAL FILES

- Grouping files into categories makes it easier to quickly find what you're looking for.
- The files you use most often should be most accessible and easily identifiable.
- Make sure your files have good homes: store them close to where you use them (kitchen as well as office) in easy-to-access units such as open-top rolling file carts and portable file holders. File cabinets—whether vertical or lateral—are fine too, as long as they are well-situated and have full-suspension, gliding drawers.

DANGER: EMPTY FILES

Trick question: What's more hazardous—a fat file folder or an empty one? Answer: An empty folder—when it's unlabeled and mixed in among full ones. Don't make the common mistake of storing extra file folders in with your filing system. Empty files not only take up valuable, limited filing space, but also create the confusing illusion that you have more active files than you actually do. Then, when you're in a hurry, it's easy to mistakenly stuff a piece of paper in an empty file located next to the one you intended to use. You may subsequently spend hours looking for a piece of paper that you're sure you filed in the right place.

If you do have plenty of extra file storage space (I don't know anyone who does), and you prefer to store file supplies there, go right ahead; just be sure to keep them together in one spot instead of mixing them throughout the system. File supplies can also be stored horizontally in their original boxes on shelves or in deep drawers with other paper supplies.

THE THREE-SPEED PURGING PROCESS

During my two decades as a professional organizer, I've gone through literally miles of piles and files with my clients. Practice makes perfect, or at least it makes an expert. Over the years, I've developed and refined an effective purging process: Three-speed purging. You see, the secret to effective paper purging is speed—specifically, three types of speed. (No, not fast-faster-fastest, although sometimes it does seem to work that way.) They are: speed sort, speed feed, and speed weed. Speed-sorting and speed-feeding are used for purging piles; speed-weeding is for purging files.

The three-speed process solves three common paperosis-causing dilemmas:

- LINGERING—spending too much time either reading stuff or staring at it while your mind goes off in 40 different directions.
- SIDETRACKING—repeatedly stopping to "do" various papers (pay a bill, fill out a form, return a call, create a new file).
- POSTPONING—putting aside things to "decide on later" (later = never).

Come along with me now and see how I help my clients speed through all kinds of piles and files.

PURGING PREP

1. I usually set a ticking timer for 10- to 15-minute increments beginning at the outset of the session; it creates a sense of urgency and is an ongoing reminder of the passage of time. Along with the timer, I set short-term goals (as described in Chapter Three).

2. The speed-sorting process is often done on the floor unless there is other open, broad, horizontal space available (an extremely rare occurrence).

3. I recommend having at least one ample, empty trash container handy. Large wastebaskets or boxes work best for this purpose. Avoid teensy, cute "guest bathroom" wastebaskets; they fill up too quickly. Plastic bags that flop over are also a waste of time (except when used as liners). You want to make it as easy as possible to throw stuff out; struggling with floppy bags and tiny baskets wastes time and effort.

● ●

The Art of Tossing

Make it easy to toss things out, and you will. Remember to treat your wastebaskets like babies: keep them within close reach at all times, feed them frequently, and change them often.

● ●

Speed Sort. This is the divide-and-conquer step for de-piling. I quickly sort any items that can be identified at a glance into "category stacks." The key here is that you're not stopping to read or or make any major decision or even think. It's almost like a game—how fast can you pull all similar items together?

Project Time

Category stacks tend to come in four styles:

Bulk: non-paper and semi-paper items that take up a lot of space.

Bits: pieces of paper in all different sizes, often with handwritten notes.

Business: letter-size and legal-size papers, mostly computer-printed or typed.

Bye-bye: stuff that's practically begging, "please toss me out!"

Category stacks vary, depending on overall pile contents. Here are some examples of typical stacks.

SAMPLE CATEGORY STACKS

Bulk:

Books, binders, notebooks, and manuals

Publications (magazines, journals, catalogs)

Supplies (office and other)

Bits:

Business cards and address/phone scraps

Notes (anything handwritten, including lists on Post-its)

Clippings (including coupons, cartoons, articles, recipes)

Business:

Bills/invoices (to pay)

Correspondence (including e-mail printouts and memos)

Financial records (including paid bills and receipts)

*ced**Bye-bye:**

Junk mail (particularly if marked "Urgent")

Ads, brochures, fliers (especially "Free Gift" offers)

Used envelopes (from bills and solicitations)

*Feel free to use your handy trash receptacles for these and any other items you feel like instantly tossing. When I'm working with a client, however, I never actually throw anything away for them. Instead, I group together all items that look tossable to show how much paper clutter is really just trash waiting to be disposed of (recycled or discarded). Sometimes after assembling a stack of old, used bill envelopes, I'll take a ruler and measure the stack to demonstrate how much space they take up. This is often a highly motivating eye-opener.

WHY SORT?

"What's the purpose of sorting?" asked a skeptical-sounding man in one of my workshops. "Isn't it just a delaying tactic?" Good point. Organizers (and other organized people) tend to assume that everyone already knows why we sort first.

Grouping similar things together helps you focus your attention so you can utilize your decision-making momentum. Unsorted clutter usually fragments your attention and makes it difficult to really "see" what you have. Think how difficult it would be to shop, for example, if supermarkets jumbled all merchandise together instead of grouping products into department categories.

But sorting *can* become a "delaying tactic," as my cynical student put it, when it's not done quickly and purposefully. If you dawdle over old junk mail or get lost reading articles you clipped ages ago, you'll spend more time dithering than de-piling. That's why the speed-sorting process is so effective: it demands both speed and focus.

● ●

Out of Sorts?

Sorting Scenario: When you try to sort your piles, you end up surrounded by dozens of mini-piles, each consisting of maybe three pieces of paper. Avoid this mini-pile dilemma by limiting your groupings to a *maximum* of 12 broad, not narrow, categories. *Important reminder: They must all be composed of items that are recognizable at a glance.* Remember, at this point you're just sorting, not making decisions or coming up with file names. If you do end up with mini-piles, look for any category overlap and, when possible, combine them. But whatever you do, avoid designating a "Miscellaneous" stack. It's too easy to just put everything in it, and you'll end up right back where you started.

● ●

SUPER SPEED-SORT SECRET

Often the quickest way to produce visible results is by first pulling out the "bulk" items (e.g., supplies, magazines, books) and collecting them into designated containers—category-labeled boxes or bins. (I use Post-its for quick, temporary labels.) Bulky stuff takes up a lot of room, often artificially inflating paper piles. Office supplies are particularly insidious pile-swellers. Extracting multiple notepads, excess binders, extra mouse-pads, etc., causes an instant-weight-loss effect on piles. Depending on how many supplies are buried in the piles, the results can be quite dramatic, with sometimes up to a 50 percent reduction of pile poundage. (For suggestions on setting up supplies storage systems that discourage overstocking, see Chapter Five.)

Once all the bulky items have been removed from the piles and categorized, we speed-sort the remaining papers into the other category stacks.

● ●

Pile Padding

Your piles are already fat enough. Do you really need to pad them?

Many piles tend to harbor at least one legal pad with only the top sheet or two used. (I once unearthed 42 pads like that from the teetering piles of a client who owned an insurance agency.) Why are these "illegal pads," as I like to call them, so common? My theory is, your brain perceives that as long as the top pages are still attached to the pad, the pages are not "papers"—they are part of a "thing," which is not as scary as loose papers.

Anyway, unless a client has a compelling argument for leaving the pads intact (I'm rarely persuaded), I detach the unused portion and put it in the Supplies container. The used pages go into the Notes category and are evaluated—and often discarded—later in the session.

● ●

Speed Feed.

Purging paper clutter is often a matter of decision making. Many piles are actually composed of postponed decisions. So during the second de-piling step, I prod clients into making a fast yet effective decision on each item—one category at a time,

one thing at a time. The speed-feed process works like this: I quickly "feed" each piece separately to them, simultaneously announcing it: "Letter from 1989!" "Newspaper clipping, undated!" "Scribbled note!" and so forth. (*Note:* I never, ever let them have more than one piece at a time. This is crucial. I've found it's almost impossible for most people to focus properly if they're holding two or more items.) I give them a few seconds to look at it and then—if they haven't discarded it or stated what they want to do with it—I prod them (verbally, not electrically) into making a decision. Then I immediately feed them the next paper.

It's a grueling yet extremely effective process. The more papers I feed them, the more they end up deciding to toss, if only to end the torture. Of course, I'm careful to never let them discard anything truly important.

After enough clients told me that they just "couldn't" make de-piling decisions without my help, I devised a decision-making exercise that they could use on their own. It's adapted from the prodding questions I most commonly ask while speed-feeding. I call it the Five Ws of Clutter Control, and you can use it to speed-feed yourself. Here's how it works.

THE FIVE Ws OF CLUTTER CONTROL

Any time you're having difficulty making a quick decision on what to do with a piece of paper, ask yourself—aloud—one or more of the following questions:

What is this?

Why would I want to keep it?

When would I ever need it?

Where would I look for it?

Who else might have it?

The Five Ws is a focusing exercise. Asking the questions out loud forces you to focus instead of letting your mind go off on time-wasting tangents.

What you're aiming for is a quick, specific answer to just one of the questions. *I've found that at least 50 percent of the time, asking just the first W provides enough reason to throw out the piece of paper.* The other 50 percent of the time, one of the other Ws helps decide whether the paper should be filed, acted on, or forwarded along (possibly to someone else's piles).

Once you've decided what to do with it, jot your decision on one corner of the paper (use a Post-it note if you don't want to mark the document itself) and put it in the most appropriate category of your paper-flow system. Of course, if you decide to toss it, you get to omit this step.

By the way, noting your decision instead of attempting to take action on it as you're de-piling helps prevent Sidetracking Syndrome.

● ●

The "Handle It Once" Myth

That old advice about "handle a piece of paper only once" just isn't working for most people. ("Once a day" may be more realistic.) I think a more effective goal is to make a decision about each piece of paper the first time you handle it. If it's a paper you want or need to keep, decide where it should go (preferably not in a pointless pile) and then mark your decision in an upper corner of the paper as described in the Five Ws of Clutter Control. This way, the next time you handle it, you'll be able to really *handle* it—or at least you'll know what needs to be done with it.

● ●

CURING SUBSCRIBITIS

Be ruthless in disposing of old magazines, journals, and newsletters you've been saving for no good reason. If your publication piles appear limitless, you may have a condition I call *Subscribitis,* which is caused by subscribing to more publications than you can possibly read in your lifetime. I've found that people who suffer from Subscribitis often have trouble letting go of "shoulds" (as in, "I really should read that...and that...and that") and "can'ts" (as in, "I just can't get rid of that—I haven't read it yet").

Curing Subscribitis is fairly simple—but that doesn't mean it's easy. There's no magic pill. It's the kind of condition where the patient must actively participate in the healing process, which involves the following steps:

1. ACCEPTING. Accept the fact that it is impossible to read everything you think you "should" read. After all, there's barely enough time to read what you have to read and what you want to read. The shoulds will always pile up. (Sadly, some people find it too painful to accept this truth and remain lifelong Subscribitis sufferers, their surroundings continually clogged by towering piles of periodicals.)

2. EVALUATING. Make a list of all your current subscriptions (dailies, weeklies, monthlies, etc.), and then evaluate each on a scale of 1 to 3. (1 = usually read it thoroughly, within a week of receiving; 2 = usually read it thoroughly, within a month of receiving; 3 = rarely get around to reading it thoroughly.)

3. EDITING. Decide on a manageable number of publications and edit your subscriptions list accordingly, eliminating all "3s" and perhaps some "2s" as well, depending on the dimensions of your list.

SUBSCRIBITIS: A condition caused by subscribing to more publications than you can possibly read in your lifetime.

Tip: I've observed that approximately one daily newspaper or bulletin plus one weekly publication plus two monthlies seems to be the maximum manageable number for many people.

4. DIVESTING. Divest yourself of excess active subscriptions. However, unsubscribing can be difficult. One way to make this step as positive and pain-free as possible is to contact each publication and request that the remainder of your issues be sent to another address (such as a library, a convalescent facility, or a school—assuming it's a G-rated magazine, of course). Another way is to remind yourself that you can now read most publications online.

5. MAINTAINING. Estimate how much weekly "reading maintenance" time you can realistically afford to spend keeping up
with all your reading, including online and books. (*Hint:* 168
hours may not be a sufficiently realistic estimate. Edit your list
again.) For inspiration, review your Household and Personal
Maintenance Checklist in Chapter Three.

THAT SINKING FEELING

"If everyone keeps stacking *National Geographics* in garages and attics instead of throwing them away, the
magazine's weight will sink the continent 100 feet
sometime soon and we will all be inundated by the
oceans." —*Journal of Irreproducible Results*

FROM MAIL TO PAIL

The increasing popularity of e-mail notwithstanding, incoming "snail
mail" continues to be a major source of paper clutter for many people. Here's how to process mail quickly:

1. Stand next to a wastebasket or recycling system. (It's been
   demonstrated that decisions are made more quickly while
   standing, especially when wearing painful shoes.)
2. With an easy-to-use letter opener (not the kind that is more
   decorative than useful), quickly slit open envelopes.
3. Immediately discard all obvious junk mail (if it's stamped "Urgent" that's usually a dead giveaway) as well as extraneous
   items such as advertising inserts and outer envelopes. *Note:*
   It's easier to adopt the habit of instantly letting go of junk
   mail than it is to get your name removed from the infinity of
   mailing lists.

4. Categorize what's left into your paper-flow or action-file system.

5. Make a conscious effort to get rid of catalogs as quickly as possible. Put any that you choose to keep in an upright holder next to a favorite reading spot; when new catalogs come in, get rid of older ones.

Tip: A Post Office box or private mail box can help keep clutter away. Whenever possible, process mail before you bring it home, getting rid of anything discardable. What remains (bills, correspondence, invitations, etc.) can be quickly categorized into sheer plastic folders in different colors. Keep some in your briefcase, totebag, or car for categorizing on the go.

CANCEL BILL-PAYING CLUTTER

There are at least three clutter-free options for bill paying:

Automatic (electronic) bill paying. More and more companies are offering this service.

Internet bill-paying. Services are offered by banks and utilities.

Bookkeeper. If you're uncomfortable with e-services, you can always hire someone to pay your bills for you.

Speed Weed.

This is the file-purging step. When I help clients weed their files, I have two rules:

Project and Maintenance Time

1. STAY FOCUSED. Remember: weeding, not reading.

2. KEEP MOVING FORWARD. No going back in the trash to rescue clutter (unless you realize you've accidentally discarded
   money, legal documents, or other valuables).

If someone gets stuck and has trouble deciding whether to refile or
toss a piece of paper, asking one or more of the following questions usually helps:

- Did you remember you had this before you looked at it just now?
- If you got rid of it, could you get it again? Would it be worth the
  trouble?
- If you keep it, will you know where to find it?
- What's the worst thing that could happen if you discarded it?
- What's the likelihood of that ever happening?

PREVENTING "PAPER HANGOVERS"

For most people, weeding files is often a grueling process. That's why I
recommend limiting it to no more than a couple of hours at a stretch,
unless you take periodic breaks. (Set the timer for 10 minutes maximum
to limit break time.) Otherwise you'll run the risk of getting what I call
a *paper hangover*. That's when the mind begins to rebel after making too
many paper-related decisions, and you start using poor judgment. If you
keep working after the onset of a paper hangover, there's a tendency to
make some unwise and ultimately regrettable decisions.

One of my clients forgot to heed this advice. One day, in a frenzy of
weeding while alone in her office, she succumbed to a paper hangover–induced urge to discard what she vaguely recalled were several
boxes of old client records. Later, as she was reviving herself with a cold
drink, the awful truth dawned on her that one of the boxes actually con-
tained all of her employee records and other important documents (in a
file labeled "Important Papers," no less). Fortunately the trash hadn't

been picked up yet, so she was able to salvage the crucial files. But she learned a valuable lesson.

WHEN TO WEED

People are always asking me, "How often should I weed my files?" The answer is, it depends. Some people swear by the "one file a day" weeding method (i.e., maintenance), while others prefer annual file purges (i.e., projects). My favorite option is the *In-Out Inventory Rule:* whenever you go to file a paper, see if you can get rid of something else from that file. Even if you only do this 50 percent of the time, it will consistently have a file-slimming impact.

TO SHRED OR NOT TO SHRED?

Paper shredders offer another potential way to get rid of clutter—or to postpone getting rid of it. Too often, good intentions pile up along with papers next to, or on top of, the shredder. Theoretically, shredders help you destroy documents containing confidential information (credit card numbers, banking transactions, legal correspondence, etc.); realistically, however, they often obstruct the letting-go process because it takes longer to feed papers into a shredder than it does to tear them up by hand or throw them into a fireplace.

Then again, some people say they enjoy using their shredders regularly, and find the process of shredding documents quite satisfying. (Not that I have actually worked with any of those people. But I have heard of them.)

So, like any process, it all depends on what works for you. If you're undecided about whether or not you should try using a shredder, here are some pros and cons:

Pros	Cons
Shreds paper	Costs money
	Takes time (you have to be careful to feed papers in straight, and remove staples and clips)
	Gets jammed

Obviously, I'm still trying to come up with additional positive reasons for having a paper shredder. Wait, I've got one: If you regularly need to destroy highly confidential documents (say, if you work for a politician), a shredder is going to be almost as vital as a coffee machine. But for people who have trouble letting go of paper, shredders are often more of a hindrance than a help.

CHAPTER WRAP-UP

- Paper clutter is denser than non-paper clutter, with more pieces per pile. This is a key reason why it often seems so overwhelming.
- Letting go of paper clutter involves two types of time: project time and maintenance time.
- The criteria for an effective system are that it must be simple, flexible, and growth-oriented.
- Filing relates to two types of paper: records, documents that need to be kept and are finite in quantity; and resources, what you don't have to keep and are available in unlimited quantity.
- Three systems help control Paperosis: time management, paper flow, and filing.
- One of the quickest ways to produce visible results when purging piles is by first speed-sorting the bulkiest items.

Conquering Stuff and Space

● ●

An essential step in letting go of clutter is dealing with stuff and space. Why? Because there is often a magnetic attraction between the stuff that fills up the most space and the spaces that attract the most stuff.

OVERVIEW

This chapter gives you methods and systems for conquering both non-paper clutter, a.k.a, "stuff," and the areas where it tends to accumulate. Many people claim they don't have enough space, but the real problem is usually caused by the excess stuff that's filling up the space. Stuff can be easier to tackle when viewed in the following contexts:

1 PASSIVE STUFF—Supplies

2 ACTIVE STUFF—Errands

3 PERPETUAL STUFF—Clothing and household

"I know what you're going to ask when I open this door," said Janice, a new client. We were standing in front of her garage. She pushed the button on the remote, and there before my eyes appeared a cavernous space filled to the ceiling with...boxes. Hundreds of cardboard storage boxes, in all different sizes and styles.

"What's in them?" I asked, feeling predictable.

Her voice lowered to a whisper, like someone sharing an intimate secret. "More boxes," she confessed, and then added—somewhat defensively—"they're all good boxes, though."

I nodded in what I hoped was an agreeable manner. "Of course they're *good*. I'm sure they never hurt anyone."

Janice looked uneasy, as though she had just remembered the purpose of our session. "Some are from wedding gifts—the pretty gold ones," she said, as though hoping I'd be swayed by this appealing description.

There was a long, meaningful pause. "So," I finally asked, "when did you get married?"

"Fourteen years ago."

 house is just a pile of stuff with a cover on it."
—*George Carlin*

TOO MUCH OF A GOOD THING?

Janice had what I call "a bad case of the goods." Like many people with clutter problems, she unthinkingly placed a much higher value on what was "good" than she did on her space, time, and sense of well-being. So here she was, paying me hundreds of dollars to help her let go of hundreds of empty boxes. (This, by the way, is not an unusual scenario.)

Earlier in these pages, I cited a quote from William Morris: "Have nothing in your houses that you do not know to be useful or believe to be beautiful." It's wise clutter-control advice—but only up to a point. The problem is, it doesn't take into account the issue of "good stuff." *Good Stuff* can be defined as "anything that is potentially useful" (such as Janice's boxes).

I've noticed that my clients and workshop participants only use the term Good Stuff for certain types of clutter—things that are difficult for them to describe or justify any other way. For example, they'll rarely refer to their clothing clutter as Good Stuff; it's always clothes or clothing. Likewise, items such as books, CDs, housewares, tools, and toys tend to be referred to specifically, not generally.* What they call Good Stuff, however, is just...stuff.

● ●

Good for What?

Whenever clients describe certain items as Good Stuff, I point out that just because stuff is good doesn't mean it's good for *them*.

● ●

Over the course of my many years in the clutter trenches, I discovered a useful way of categorizing Good Stuff. I gradually noticed that it comes in two main varieties: passive and active. Passive stuff involves supplies of all kinds—products that need to be stored and periodically replenished. Active stuff relates to errand-type items—things that need to have something done to them and/or be taken somewhere else. I also observed that there's only one thing that both types of Good Stuff have in common: There always seems to be way too much of these things.

The Good Stuff Checklist on the next page identifies the most common types of accumulations in both categories. Feel free to check off the ones that are creating clutter for you.

"We tend to confuse the good life with a life of goods."
—*Simon Schama*

*Except when they are all smushed together in, say, a closet or garage; then I often hear this description: "There's really a lot of Good Stuff in there."

GOOD STUFF CHECKLIST

Passive/Supplies

_____ Boxes (gift boxes, shipping boxes, in-case-we-need-to-return-it boxes)

Packing materials (Styrofoam peanuts, bubble wrap, shredded paper)

_____ Bags (paper and plastic grocery bags, department store bags, gift bags)

_____ Gift wrapping (new and used wrapping paper, ribbons, and bows)

_____ Duplicates or multiples of just about every type of supplies (office, cleaning, cooking, etc.)

Active/Errands

_____ Stuff to be returned (to stores or friends)

_____ Stuff to recycle (bottles, cans, newspapers)

_____ Stuff to be repaired

_____ "Stuff I'd like to sell if I have a garage sale"

_____ "Stuff to be donated—I just haven't gotten around to it"

PERPETUAL STUFF

Passive and active items aren't the only types of stuff that are considered good. There's also *perpetual stuff*—namely, clothing and most household-related items. As mentioned earlier, I've noticed that these tend to be referred to by their owners in a different, more specific way. (I can't say for sure, but I suspect it's because clothing and housewares may appear more obviously useful. They are not like, say, lots of boxes, or stacks of recyclables, which often actually resemble trash; or excessive amounts of supplies, which can look pretty ridiculous.)

In Chapter Two's Clutter Categories Checklist, there are 10 types of Clothing and Accessories items listed along with 18 types of Household items. Not surprisingly, a lot of perpetual stuff seems magnetically attracted to certain spaces, namely, closets and garages—areas mentioned in two of the Top 10 Clutter Questions.

Letting go of all the different kinds of stuff is a process that's different from purging paper, although there are similarities too. The most important difference is that, unlike paper, stuff has no "records" equivalent. Essentially, stuff is all like "resources": Virtually none of the excess stuff you're keeping actually has to be kept (the IRS certainly doesn't care about it*). You're only hanging on to it because you haven't been ready to let go of it... until now, of course.

The paper and stuff decluttering processes are similar in that both prevention and purging are necessary for letting go of most kinds of clutter. But because of how paper clutter and stuff clutter differ—namely, paper clutter is condensed and stuff clutter is bulky—the order of the processes differs. As explained in the previous chapter, paper purging is best done after the systems for prevention are in place. Stuff, however, usually should be purged prior to creating storage (prevention) systems.

---

*Unless you donate it and claim it as a deduction. That's why it's wise to get a receipt when you donate stuff.

ABOUT PURGING AND PREVENTION

- Purging is about making the choice—quickly and effectively—to get rid of existing obstructions.
- Prevention involves establishing storage systems and maintenance procedures (or rules) for the stuff you decide to keep.

FIVE STEPS FOR ELIMINATING STUFF

I've found that all three types of stuff respond well to the following five-step purging program.

1. Set aside a specific block of *uninterrupted* time for your decluttering project. Make sure that the phone, doorbell, TV, etc., will not create distractions. Anywhere from one to three hours or more at a time is good, depending upon your energy level and the size of the project. Set a ticking, kitchen-type timer to keep you on track; it can really help you stay focused. You'll also need to set aside subsequent "errand time" to help you deal with items you uncover that may need to be taken to the cleaner, recycler, repair shop, etc.

2. Decide exactly which area you're going to concentrate on for the allotted time period. Be realistic: If you have a lot of clutter, it's unlikely you'll be able to go through all of it in one session. Choose an attainable goal that will enable you to see results by the time your timer buzzes. For example, if you have a clutter-filled garage, focus on clearing one section at a time. If you have lots of boxes, crates, and/or bags (or other types of containers) filled with "miscellaneous," count them and decide how many you can tackle at a time.

3. Obtain six roomy boxes or plastic laundry baskets (square or rectangular) and label them (with stick-on labels): To Clean; Give Away/Sell; Recycle; Repair; Return; Keep. (*Note:* Different situations may need different category names, or different numbers or sizes of containers.) Also, have a good-sized wastebasket or trash pail, not just a bag, on hand.

"I did not have 3000 pairs of shoes. I had 1060."
—*Imelda Marcos*

4. Pick up only one item at a time, and decide which labeled container to put it in. Your goal should be to put as many things as possible in the wastebasket, "Give Away/Sell," and "Recycle" containers. Ask yourself, "How well could I live without this?" each time you find yourself wavering. Another indecision-buster is, "Is this item more trouble to keep than it's worth to me?" Items that do end up in the "Keep" box should be individually labeled, using removable stickers, with instructions such as "Kitchen—under sink" or "Office—bookcase," unless you feel it is obvious where the item should be put.

5. When the labeled containers are full, you should distribute the contents as follows:
   - **TO CLEAN:** Put washables in your laundry hamper; bag items to be dry cleaned, label the bag "Dry Cleaning," and take it to the dry cleaner within 48 hours (or have someone take it for you).
   - **GIVE AWAY/SELL:** Use the same process described for "To Clean," modified for this purpose. Be honest about whether you will get around to having a garage sale anytime in the near future; it may be ultimately more profitable for you to donate saleable items to a charity—espe-

cially if they'll haul the stuff away for you—and get a receipt for a tax write-off.

- RECYCLE: Depending upon whether you have curbside recycling in your area or if you have to take the stuff to a recycling center (or call someone to pick it up), it can be as simple as sorting it into the curbside containers or as laborious as loading it into your vehicle and, as with the dry cleaning, getting it out within 48 hours.

- REPAIR: Think about whether certain items are worth repairing or whether it might be better to just donate them to charity and buy something more up to date. If you do decide on the repair option, then figure out where you're going to take the item(s) to have them fixed. Then, out to the car, and get it done within 48 hours.

- RETURN: Follow the same procedure as in "Repair."

- KEEP: Carry the "Keep" box/basket from room to room, putting away items as you go. Always put things as near as possible to where they'll be used, and use hard-to-reach storage areas only for infrequently used items. If any drawers, shelves, etc., are already too full to add anything to them, ask yourself which items you can get rid of: the ones in the "Keep" basket, or some of the ones that are filling up the space where you want to put the items from the "Keep" basket? Something's got to go! And if you're keeping too many things, using the favorite excuse of "I might need this some day," keep in mind that you can always get more stuff but you can never get more time. So stop wasting your valuable time by keeping too much stuff!

"Junk is stuff we throw away; stuff is junk we keep."
—*Anonymous*

BE CREATIVE IN YOUR SOLUTIONS TO STORAGE PROBLEMS

As you sort through your items to keep and look for places to put everything, be creative. First, you might sort items into five categories by frequency of use:

1. *At least daily*—underwear, toothpaste/brush, hair dryer, etc.
2. *At least weekly*—favorite outfits, exercise wear, and shoes
3. *At most monthly*—special occasion outfits, jewelry, certain shoes
4. *Rarely, if ever*—formal wear (i.e., tuxedos, costumes)
5. *Seasonally*—snowsuits, ski wear, gloves, hats, swimsuits

While deciding where to store these things, keep in mind the following general rules:

- The stuff you use the most often should be easiest to access.
- Keep infrequently used items in clear plastic containers (shoe boxes/sweater boxes) so you can see the contents and not forget what you have. If you don't use see-through containers, label everything clearly.
- Use a row or rows of hooks on the backs of doors or even on an open wall space to make it easy to hang things up. This can be especially helpful to people who often leave clothes on the floor.
- Layer shallow baskets in deep drawers for underwear, socks, and accessories. Frequently used items should be on the top layer.

SWIMMING IN SUPPLIES

For the most part, supplies are specific groups of items that are needed to sustain or maintain various systems and activities. As anyone who has ever shopped knows, there are many different types of supplies, and any one of them can be a clutter source.

Take another look at the Supplies section of the Clutter Categories Checklist in Chapter Two to see which types of supplies are contributing to your clutter. The main difference between supplies and other types of stuff is that supplies are meant to be replenished periodically as they are used up. Clutter problems surface when supplies are over-replenished repeatedly. Acquiring more supplies when your space is already filled up with them is like pouring water into a bucket that's already full. No wonder so many people tell me they feel like they're "drowning in clutter."

One of these people was Janice, my "boxaholic" client. Here's the process I used to save her (and many other similarly afflicted folks) from getting "stuffocated" by Good Stuff, such as boxes, bags, and arts and crafts materials, all of which have a well-documented tendency to accumulate far faster than they can be used. *Note:* These steps can also be adapted for conquering other types of passive clutter.

● ●

The Best Places for Storing Supplies

There are special places designed to store many, many supplies. These places are called "stores."

● ●

PRUNING PASSIVE CLUTTER

1. IDENTIFY WHICH TYPE(S) OF SUPPLIES ARE CREATING A CLUTTER PROBLEM. In Janice's case, of course, boxes were a key component. Your case might be different (or not); review your Clutter Categories Checklist in Chapter Two so you can focus on your specific supplies issues.

2. CHOOSE THE BEST PLACE(S) TO KEEP THEM. When deciding, remember that it's usually best to locate your supplies as close as possible to where they will actually be used. Frequency

of use should also influence location: Store the supplies you need to access most often in the most accessible spots; infrequently used supplies can be relegated to your home's equivalent of Siberia.

I asked Janice how often she actually used any boxes, and she admitted that it wasn't more than about five times a year—and then she usually had to go and buy a shipping box because she had trouble finding the right size or type in her box jungle. (However, she wasn't ready to just get rid of all of them; she wanted to have a "reasonable number" on hand so she could have the option of using some.)

● ●

Where It Works, Not Where It Fits

Don't just put things where they fit. Put them where they'll work best to save you time and effort.

● ●

3. DECIDE HOW MUCH SPACE YOU WISH TO DEVOTE TO SUPPLIES STORAGE. Next, I asked Janice how much space she wanted to use for her box collection. Never having thought about it before, she didn't know what to answer. So I offered her some choices. My method is to start with the absurd. In this case, I said, "How do you feel about just continuing to use the entire garage as a home for your boxes?" Her response was swift—"No!" "OK, how about half the garage?" "Hmmm.... No." "Well, what about a quarter of the garage?" "Mmmaybe.... No."

Finally, I got her to suggest that maybe two shelves' worth of boxes was sufficient. Coming to that conclusion on her own was an important milestone. We could then move on to the next step.

4. **CATEGORIZE AND CONSOLIDATE.** Look over your supplies and group together all similar items. In the case of Janice's boxes, we removed all the boxes that were nested inside other boxes, spread them out (it was quite a landscape), and then grouped them into categories (by size and type). Once she could see how many of each kind she'd accumulated, she was ready for the next step.

5. **PURGE EXCESS BY LIMITING QUANTITY.** I often use the "pick-a-number tactic," asking the client to choose a specific number of items from each category or subcategory, and then seeing whether the chosen space will accommodate them. For example, Janice initially decided that three of each type of box would be "manageable," so we pared down the excess to that number. But there were still too many boxes to fit on the shelves allocated for box storage, so she changed the limit to two of each and pared again.

   This process can be quite educational for anyone who has never really thought about how many of a particular kind of item can fit comfortably into a specific space or area. Becoming conscious of the limits of your space makes you less likely to overstock and exceed your boundaries. (*Note:* This step is especially important if you are a boxaholic with an overabundance of "in-case boxes," that is, appliance boxes you've been keeping in case you need to return something or in case you move.)

● ●

Pick a Number . . .

The pick-a-number tactic makes the issue of letting go of particular items less of a focus. By shifting your attention from your discomfort at the possibility of getting rid of stuff to realistic options for storing what's left, the process becomes easier.

● ●

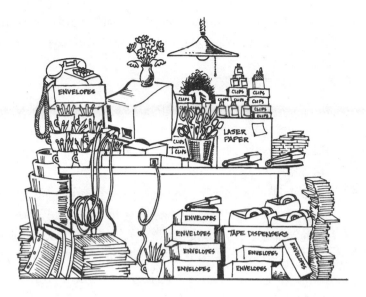

OVERSTOCKED OFFICE SUPPLIES: Stockpiling little boxes of paper clips, multiple pads of Post-It notes, reams of paper, mugs crammed with pens...

OVERCOMING OVERSTOCKED
OFFICE SUPPLIES

Of all the different types of passive stuff, there's one that seems to plague just about everyone nowadays: office supplies.

Overloading on office supplies is easy to do since many of the products seem inexpensive; yet they add up quickly, and they can take up a lot of space. But what I find particularly sad is the wasted time-saving potential; if extra office supplies are put in the right places, they can be a help instead of a hindrance.

So, if you've been stockpiling little boxes of paperclips, multiple pads of Post-it notes, reams of paper, mugs crammed with pens, not to mention all those legal pads...the time has come to deal with them! Here's how:

1. Group all similar items together (pens with pens, tape with tape, etc.) so you can see at a glance how much you have of each type of supply.

2. Count up the different places where you tend to do any kind of paperwork (e.g., process mail, pay bills, clip coupons, look at catalogs, read). The kitchen, dining table, family room, bedroom, bathroom, home office, and car are all popular paper-processing and piling places.

3. For each of your "paper magnet" areas, assemble one small container—a 6-inch-diameter basket is fine—of commonly used office supplies (pencil/pen, notepad, highlighter, scissors, stapler, paper-clips, Post-its). The supplies you choose for these "mini-offices" should be ones that you've wished were handy but never have been—until now.

4. Allocate a limited space (an out-of-the way drawer or a banker's box) for storing back-up supplies.

5. Donate whatever supplies are left to a nonprofit organization, a school, or wherever is most convenient. Then at least they will do someone else some good—unless, of course, you've waited too long and the pens have dried up, the paperclips are rusted, and the envelope flaps are stuck closed, all of which happens when you overstock these supplies.

CONTROLLING CANINE AND CAT CLUTTER

If you are one of the millions of Americans who are owned by a cat (59 million) or a dog (52.9 million) or any combination of the two, chances are your pet supplies are contributing to the massive passive clutter in your home. Pet food and grooming products are common clutter culprits, as are toys; but they can be kept in check by using a few simple tools and rules:

- Designate a specific area for pet supplies storage. Otherwise it's easy to end up losing track of all the places you've squirreled stuff away (pardon the pun) and stockpiling too much. Ideally, the area you choose should be more easily accessible to you than to your pet(s).

- A rolling cart made of plastic, stackable bins and/or drawers can work well as a designated "pet supply center." (These carts are usually available for under $20 at discount department stores.) A large, deep bottom drawer is a good place to store pet toys or cat litter. A scoop can be stored with the cat litter for easy access. Other drawers can be used for things like grooming supplies, medications, and food tins.

- For accessible, effective cabinet storage of dry pet food, clear plastic cereal containers with flip-top lids take the chore out of pouring and prevent soggy snacks. Another plus: since the contents are visible, you'll know when you're running low. (And guess what? These containers are great for storing "people food" too.) But, if your cabinets are too cluttered for you to add anything like this, read on.

CLEARING OUT CLUTTER CAVES

Kitchens and bathrooms attract various kinds of passive stuff, perhaps because both of these rooms invariably harbor "clutter caves"—better known as cabinets.

For example, look inside most medicine cabinets and you'll find a lot more than medicine. Seems like everything winds up in there, crammed onto those skinny little shelves: Cosmetics and toiletries, shaving materials, dental and hair-care items, contact lens solution, sunscreen, cleaning products... stuff that seems to breed. Of course, whatever doesn't fit usually ends up in the cabinet under the sink, or gets spread out over the counters and any other available surfaces. The same thing happens in kitchens, except the supplies involved tend to be more edible. Also, kitchen cabinets are apt to contain more types of perpetual stuff, such as cooking and eating utensils and various appliances (many forgotten or rarely used).

But all is not lost—at least, it won't be if you follow this simple four-step process for clearing out these clutter caves.

Steps for Conquering Cabinet Clutter

1. CLEAR OUT. Remove the contents of each cabinet (one cabinet at a time); jettison old and/or ineffective supplies and products. This includes all those tiny, bewitching bottles of hotel toiletries, cute little containers of jam (from gift baskets or room service), and shriveled packets of ketchup or other take-out condiments.

2. CATEGORIZE. Group remaining items into categories, e.g., (bathroom) cosmetics, dental, hair care, medications; (kitchen) canned goods, glassware/mugs, cleaning products, cookware.

3. CONTEMPLATE. Do all of these items really belong in your cabinets? Think about which ones you use most often and where you actually like to use them; then transfer nonessentials to more appropriate areas (e.g., a donation bin or perhaps the trash).

4. CLUSTER. Use narrow rectangular containers, preferably transparent, for easily accessible storage of products often used in tandem. For example, in the bathroom: skin care (cleanser/moisturizer/toner), dental care (toothpaste/mouthwash/floss), shaving supplies (razor/shaving cream/aftershave).

IT'S ALL IN THE PACKAGING

One way to cut down on bathroom and kitchen clutter is to get in the habit of discarding inefficient packaging from various products you buy and replacing it with reusable, convenient containers and dispensers. Look for clear plastic canisters that can be used for a variety of supplies (personal hygiene products; cereals and pasta; anything you need to access regularly).

ATTACKING ACTIVE CLUTTER

A certain amount of clutter is caused by active stuff that has gotten stuck in various stages of transition. Active stuff is supposed to be moving—specifically, out. It is the stuff of which errands are made.

TYPICAL ERRANDS
(STUFF TO TAKE SOMEWHERE)

THINGS THAT ARE GOING AWAY PERMANENTLY ...

_____ Outgoing mail

_____ Packages to be shipped

_____ Purchases to return (or exchange)

Books and magazines to return (and/or donate) to library

_____ Video rentals to return

_____ Items to donate to charitable organization

_____ Stuff to be recycled

THINGS THAT ARE GOING AWAY BUT SHOULD COME BACK ...

_____ Clothes to be dry-cleaned or altered

_____ Shoes to be repaired

_____ Other things to be repaired

_____ Film to be developed or duplicated

_____ Stuff to be shared with friends, neighbors, family, coworkers

Remember, errands are like dogs: they need to be run regularly—or at least taken outside—otherwise they create messes inside your home.

CREATING AN EFFECTIVE ERRANDS SYSTEM

If you recognize any errands items as clutter sources, you need a good maintenance system for managing them. An errands system has two basic components:

1. A designated area
2. A time limit

Designated Area

Your errands system can be located wherever it works best for you. You may have to experiment until you find the right place. I have found that the most effective place is often near the door you use most, which is usually either the front door or the door leading to where vehicles are kept.

The physical part of the system consists of a small table or tiered rolling cart for holding items that need to go out. Square or rectangular containers (round or oval shapes are less space-efficient) often work well in conjunction with the table or cart, especially when labeled with your most frequently used errand categories. Tote baskets with fold-down handles, like the ones used in stores, can be especially handy for transporting various errand loads.

Tip: The errands area is also a good place to designate a "landing strip" for frequently used and often misplaced items such as keys and sunglasses; keep a pen or pencil and a pad of Post-it notes there, too, for jotting quick reminders.

I've actually had some clients express concern that having an errands area by the main door might look "too messy." These are usually the people who have piles of stuff everywhere else. I'll say to them, "Messy compared to what?!" But this can become a legitimate concern if you keep putting stuff by the front door and it never goes out. Which is why the second component of any effective errands system is the time limit you impose on yourself.

Time Limit

The trick here is to establish a rule: Anything that gets put in the errands area must go out* within a set period of time. *Hint:* One year is not a good "set period of time," unless you want your errands area to become a clutter pit. I recommend a one-week limit—maximum. The best way to enforce this rule is to schedule regular maintenance time for errands in your time management system or calendar.

Some people prefer to run all their errands on weekends, while others manage to do them during the week, depending on their schedules. Whichever way works for you is fine, as long as you are able to get your errands done regularly. Another option: pay someone to do your errands for you. (If you don't know anyone you could hire for this purpose, check your local Yellow Pages under Errands or Personal Services.) *Note:* Those labeled baskets will make it easier for you to delegate errand tasks.

---

*"Go out" does not mean "stuff it in the car and hope it gets to its destination by itself." Unless, of course, you don't mind having a clutter-mobile.

ERRANT ERRANDS

What if you notice that eventually, despite regular maintenance efforts, your errands area has somehow managed to turn into a clutter swamp? I've observed several ways in which people commonly sabotage their errands systems:

1. Allowing the designated area to become a sort of purgatory for postponed decisions, such as . . .
   - Purchases you're not sure you want to return
   - Items to be repaired that might not be worth fixing
   - Stuff you keep changing your mind about whether to donate or not

If postponed decisions are at the root of any stale items, pick up each item separately, look it over and ask yourself: What's the worst thing that might happen, realistically, if this vanished tomorrow? Depending on your answer, you can choose one of the following options:

- Discard or donate it.
- Put an "expiration date" on it (with a Post-it note) for one week maximum from today and make a corresponding note in your time management system. When that date rolls around, if the item is still in the errands area; discard or donate the item.

2. Memory lapses, such as . . .
   - Things you keep forgetting to give back to your friend or relative who you only see occasionally
   - Stuff you never seem to get around to taking wherever it needs to go

If memory lapses are to blame for any of the errand-area buildup, you need to start making reminder notes in your time management system about these items. Also, putting a Post-it note reminder at eye level by the door can help. Just don't end up overusing this method unless you want to have a Post-it-encrusted entryway. *Tip:* If you just can't seem to remember to give something to someone when you see them, go ahead and mail it to them (insure it if necessary).

3. Turning the errands area into a dumping ground for things that don't really belong there, such as . . .
   - Anything that doesn't have a designated destination (dry cleaner, library, etc.) and deadline for getting there
   - Too many "miscellaneous" items in the landing strip area (which should be restricted primarily to keys, sunglasses, pen or pencil, and Post-it pad)
   - Excess outerwear and/or accessories (hats, gloves, scarves, purses, shoes, jackets)

If the active stuff in your errands area has been superseded by passive or perpetual stuff, make a list of the types of things that seem to wind up there. Then see if you can come up with any options to either accommodate these items or prevent them from settling there. For example, if clothing and accessories consistently clog the area, consider putting up several hooks on the back of the nearby door or any appropriate wall space. A standing coatrack or hatrack is another possibility.

Remember, the less stuff you acquire and the more you let go of, the less errand-clutter you'll need to deal with.

AT A GLANCE: ERRANDS SYSTEM SET-UP

1. Set up your errands system by putting a small table or rolling cart by the exit door you use the most. You might also want to have a few containers labeled for your errand categories.
2. Schedule weekly maintenance time for doing errands, or arrange for someone to run errands for you.

EXCAVATING CLUTTER CAVERNS

Sometimes the reason your errands system keeps getting clogged up is because a nearby closet has become a "clutter cavern," overstuffed and overflowing with outerwear or other items. If that's the root of the problem, then forget about putting up hooks or a hatrack (as previously suggested). It would be like putting a Band-aid on a bullet wound.

Any of your cluttered closets can be excavated effectively by following the Five Steps for Eliminating Stuff provided earlier in this chapter.

If you have trouble letting go of clothing and accessories, apply this one rule each time you get stuck in the process: *Keep the item only if it makes you both look good and feel good now.* (Not one or the other, but both.) *Now* is a key word here. When it comes to clothing, the past and the future tend to crowd out the present. Let go of clothes that used to make you look and feel good, and clothes that you think will fit "someday." *Note:* Chapter Seven has additional suggestions for weeding clothing clutter.

● ●
The In/Out Inventory Rule

Here's an effective maintenance rule for keeping closets and other areas clutter-free: Every time you bring an item into your home, choose another similar item to let go of (something from the same category). For example, when you get a new pair of shoes, go through your shoe collection to pick out a pair that hasn't been worn in ages; then put it in the donations section of your errands system.

● ●

A GAME PLAN FOR THE GARAGE

OK, you've finally got your Good Stuff—supplies and errands items—under control. You've even cleared out your various clutter caves and caverns. Now perhaps you're ready to tackle your garage. Except for one tiny problem: like Janice, you can hardly even get into your garage, thanks to a bad case of *garagea clutteritis.*

Don't panic. Here are some steps you can take to clear it out without using dynamite. (*Note:* These steps also work for decluttering other large spaces such as attics, basements, and storage units, as well as over-stuffed bedrooms, livingrooms, etc.)

1. FOCUS. Think about how you currently use your garage versus how you'd prefer to be using it. For example, maybe you currently use it for storage, but you'd like to be able to do woodworking or crafts projects there. Decide how you want to use the space, and then sketch out a rough plan.
2. INVENTORY. Use the accompanying Garage Inventory Checklist to help you create a "before and after" plan for the specific types of things that you plan to keep or remove from your garage.
3. DEADLINE. Set a deadline for getting the job done, and block out time on your calendar or planner for the Garage Project. Be realistic; you may need to arrange for assistance (family, friend, or paid helper). Use the Space Decluttering Action Plan form provided to help you with this step.

Tip: If you tie your deadline to an event such as a neighborhood multifamily yard sale, you'll have a better shot at achieving your goal.

SPACE DECLUTTERING ACTION PLAN

Project(s) Description: _____

_____

Estimated Time: _____

Time Block(s): _____

Starting Date: _____

Target Completion Date: _____

SUPPLIES CHECKLIST

_____ protective gloves

_____ marking pens

_____ trash bags

_____ trash bins/dumpsters

_____ storage boxes

_____ storage bins

_____ _____

_____ _____

_____ _____

_____ _____

_____ _____

_____ _____

GARAGE INVENTORY CHECKLIST

Below is a list of items frequently stored in garages. (Several spaces are also provided so you can add other items. Please be specific; "Miscellaneous" is too general!)

There are two blanks provided in front of each item, for Before and After. Put a checkmark (√) in the Before column by each item that currently resides in your garage; then put a checkmark (√) in the After column next to the items that you plan to actually keep in the garage, and an "X" next to the ones you plan to eliminate.

Before	After	Inventory
_____	_____	Archived files (old tax records, etc.)
_____	_____	Bicycle(s)
_____	_____	Camping Gear
_____	_____	Car(s)
_____	_____	Clothing, off-season
_____	_____	Clothing, old/extra
_____	_____	Furniture
_____	_____	Gardening tools and equipment
_____	_____	Laundry area (washer/dryer, etc.)
_____	_____	Memorabilia
_____	_____	Sports equipment (golf, skiing, etc.)
_____	_____	Suitcases and travel items
_____	_____	Tools and workshop items
_____	_____	_____
_____	_____	_____

QUESTION: WHEN IS A GARAGE SALE NOT A GARAGE SALE?

Answer: When it's a "garage sale someday." Have you been saying for years that you're going to have a garage sale someday? (Someday is not the day that comes after Saturday.) In the meantime, you keep hanging on to, and accumulating, stuff for your imaginary sale. The most common excuse: "It's too valuable to donate."

Set a deadline, enlist the help of others, and see if you can change "someday" into Sunday.

4. PREPARE. Assemble supplies you'll need to make the decluttering go smoothly. Use the Supplies Checklist on the Space Decluttering Action Plan form to help you with this step. You might also consider renting a Dumpster if you have a huge amount of stuff to dispose of. (A bulldozer is optional.)

● ●

A Perfect Solution?

According to an article in the *Boston Globe,* buyer demand is causing home builders and designers to make three-car garages a more affordable and attainable option. But, as one home-building executive noted, the three bays aren't necessarily holding cars. Mostly, it's "stuff people don't know what to do with" that's hiding behind those doors, he said. And since home buyers would rather hide this stuff than expose it with an open garage door, builders are now designing three-bay garages with only two doors.

● ●

5. DIG IN. Now you're ready to begin the physical job of decluttering and organizing. First, allocate two holding areas (outside

the garage, if necessary) designated for "keep" and "don't keep" items. (The area allocated for "don't keep" should be at least twice as big as the "keep" area.) Your objective: fill up the "don't-keep" section.

You may want to subdivide this section with three or more large containers (boxes or bins) labeled "trash," "donate," "sell," or any other relevant subcategories. Try to make your system as simple as possible; creating too many options is counterproductive.

Next, choose a path: Decide whether you want to work around the perimeters going clockwise or counterclockwise, saving the middle for last (the Hostess cupcake method), or if you'd prefer a de-layering process (the Orco approach). Whichever way you choose, what really matters is that you plow forward systematically instead of jumping back and forth between areas.

Finally, set a ticking timer for small increments (5, 10, or 15 minutes) to help ward off Sidetracking Syndrome.

THE ONE-A-DAY RULE

Each day, make a conscious effort to let go of at least one unit of clutter. The "unit" can be one item or one containerful. For example, I once received a letter from someone who had taken my workshop six months before. She wrote: "Ever since taking your Letting Go of Clutter class, I've been getting rid of one shopping bag full of clutter each day. I'm really starting to see progress!"

So, whether it's a bag-, a box-, or a drawerful, or even just an individual piece of stuff (an empty box or an empty bag), if you let go of clutter consistently, you'll start seeing progress too. And you'll notice something else: it feels good to let go!

CHAPTER WRAP-UP

- Just because an item is "good" doesn't mean it's good for you.
- Unlike certain types of paper clutter, non-paper "stuff" has no IRS-issued rules; so, technically, you are free to let go of anything you own.
- Supplies are specific groups of items that are needed to sustain or maintain various systems and activities, and they are meant to be replenished periodically as they are used up.
- Errands are like dogs: they need to be run regularly, or else they end up making messes in the house.
- Clothing and accessories are easier to part with if you apply this rule: Keep it only if it makes you look good *and* feel good now.
- When decluttering a space such as a garage, decide whether you want to work around the perimeters, saving the middle for last (the Hostess cupcake method) or if you'd prefer a de-layering process (the Oreo approach); avoid jumping back and forth between areas.

Shedding Sentimental Clutter

● ●

A vital step in the letting go of clutter process is learning how to manage memorabilia. Why? Because when you let go of objects that remind you of memories you'd rather forget, you make room for the things that matter most to you.

OVERVIEW

This chapter offers you options and ideas for dealing with sentimental objects of all kinds. Personal memorabilia is often difficult to part with because we feel emotionally and/or historically connected to it. But you can start taking control of your sentimental stuff by recognizing the two main ways in which it affects you:

1 POSITIVE—Evokes pleasant or poignant memories

2 NEGATIVE—Stirs up stressful or uncomfortable emotions

"What do you plan to do with these?"

I was pointing to a pile of pink-and-white birth announcements I'd just uncovered while decluttering a client's "junk room." She stared at them, apparently transfixed by memories, and sighed. "Oh...I never finished sending them out."

"That's OK," I assured her. "How old is your baby now?"

"Four."

After letting this sink in, I pointed out that it was highly unlikely she would ever "finish" sending them out at this late date. (There appeared to be around 200 in the stack.) Reluctantly, she agreed. So I suggested that she discard all but one or two of them.

"No!" she gasped, recoiling as though I had just advised discarding her four-year-old. "I couldn't do that."

"Why not?"

Gazing lovingly at the stack, she whispered, "They're so...pretty." No matter how I tried to reason with her ("How about getting rid of half of them? No? OK, what about 50? 25?"), she simply wouldn't let go of even one, let alone the whole stack. So we ended up adding them to her ever-expanding "memory museum," where I'm sure they reside to this day, as pretty as ever.

●   ●   ●

Hoping this tale would at least inspire someone else to let go of similar "clutterabilia," I recounted it to another client. He laughed uproariously at the idea of anyone keeping birth announcements for that long. "Unbelievable," he muttered, shaking his head in disbelief, as I described how the other client had refused to part with so much as a single one.

Then we came across a stack of announcements from when he had received his doctorate. They were almost 10 years old. "So," I said with a grin, "what do you plan to do with these?"

You can probably guess.

Déjà vu all over again.

ARE YOU A MEMORABILIAC?

My point in telling you about these incidents is to illustrate how easy it is to let go of sentimental stuff—as long as it's not *your* stuff! Of course, letting go of your own personal memorabilia, especially if you're a sentimental soul, tends to be a whole lot harder than getting rid of other people's stuff.

As a sentimental person myself, I'm sympathetic to those who find the process painful. But I also know how important it is to manage your mementos so they don't keep cluttering up your life. Otherwise, you run the risk of becoming a *memorabiliac:* someone who accumulates vast amounts of personal memorabilia.

THE MEANING OF MEMORABILIA

To make sure we're on the same wavelength here, I want to clarify what I mean by personal memorabilia. I'm not talking about "collectible memorabilia," which involves collecting antique (or antique-looking) knickknacks. Personal memorabilia means the things we keep that evoke personal reminiscences, pleasant feelings, bittersweet emotions, and/or a sense of historical connectedness. It's the stuff that we think of as "priceless" because it often has value only to us; that's why it's the stuff that's missed most when people lose everything in a fire or other disaster.

There are a number of creative ways to categorize, organize, and/or display sentimental stuff, such as scrapbooks, photo albums, and shadow boxes—none of which will be covered here. Although these options can turn into satisfying hobbies, they are more likely to become stressful "procrastination projects" for those who are already overwhelmed by clutter and commitments.

In my experience, there are three types of memorabiliacs: Type 1 is someone who actually creates and maintains scrapbooks, photo albums, or other systems for keeping sentimental stuff in order. Type 2 is someone who aspires to being a Type 1, but rarely (if ever) gets around to creating or maintaining those systems. Type 3 is someone who has no Type 1 aspirations.

Which type are you?

If you identify yourself as a Type 1, that's admirable. But as time goes on, you may find yourself accumulating mementos (and scrapbook supplies) faster than you can capture them in your systems. The rules and steps detailed in this chapter are designed to help you deal with any existing overflow and prevent more from building up.

If you are a Type 2, the most important step you can take now is to be honest with yourself about your priorities and interests. Accept that it is OK if you never do get around to putting your stuff in scrapbooks "someday." (But you may be able to get someone else to do it for you! See Appendix B for resources.) Please let go of any pressure you've put on yourself that this project is something you "should" do. There are other ways to master your memorabilia, and we'll be covering them.

Finally, if you see yourself as a Type 3, your challenges may be simpler—not easier, just simpler. It all depends on how much sentimental clutter you've accumulated so far, and how much of it you ultimately end up keeping. That's why the following rules and techniques are designed to help make your memento-related challenges easier.

MEMORIES ARE MADE OF THIS . . . AND THIS . . . AND THIS . . .

It's easy to spend a lot of time organizing and cataloguing sentimental stuff. Your objective, however, is to focus on letting go of certain things so you don't have to spend as much time deciding where to put them. Of course, I do expect you to keep some memorabilia, but only those items that survive the rigorous testing procedures I'll be describing in a moment.

First, however, I want to clarify my three-part process for managing memorabilia. I'm going to show you how to:

1. Let go of anything that doesn't touch you in a positive or poignant way
2. Save only what you have space for
3. Keep your meaningful mementos in simple, easy-to-maintain systems

The best way to begin is by gathering together all the things you think you're keeping for sentimental reasons. However, you can also use this process on an item-by-item basis as you come across individual mementos.

SENTIMENTAL, ORNAMENTAL, OR ACCIDENTAL?

Sometimes there are things we think we're keeping for sentimental reasons that are actually not mementos at all. Such "memorabilia imposters" include:

- Antique or old knickknacks that have no real personal history (as opposed to inherited items or gifts). By all means, keep any items like this that you really, really like, as long as you have a place to display them. Otherwise, get rid of them (sell, donate, or give as gifts).
- Outdated but nonhistorical legal documents (wills, divorce papers, deeds, lawsuits, IOUs). You might want to check with your attorney before destroying any of these. In the meantime, they can be archived with your old tax papers (as described in Chapter Four).

- Old résumés and appointment books/calendars. Likewise, if you choose to keep these for historical purposes, they can be stored in your archive files (assuming you haven't run out of space yet).
- Invitations and announcements that you're only keeping as samples for design ideas. If you really think you're likely to revisit these items, set up an Invitation Samples file (or use whatever file name works for you) under the Personal category. Otherwise, the "round file" may be the best place for them.

MANAGING MEMORABILIA

Let Go of Anything That Doesn't Touch You in a Positive or Poignant Way

To do this, it's useful to first inventory your sentimental objects and papers by separating them into four categories: *Happy, Sad, Good,* and *Bad.*

HAPPY: Mementos of positive accomplishments, joyous occasions, fun times, and loving relationships, such as:

_____ Announcements and invitations (weddings, anniversaries, births, graduations, degrees, etc.)

_____ Awards and honors (certificates, trophies, plaques, merit badges, medallions, ribbons, etc.)

_____ Books (from childhood, or any volumes that have been particularly influential and meaningful to you)

_____ Cards and letters

_____ Children's stuff (report cards, artwork, etc.)

_____ Clothing and accessories ("lucky" clothes, favorite old things, costumes, uniforms)

The Four Categories of Sentimental Objects

_____ Entertainment-related (sports or arts events' ticket stubs, programs, celebrity-autographed items, etc.)

_____ Family history (genealogical materials, old documents, military or war records, etc.)

_____ Jewelry

_____ Personal publicity

_____ Photos, slides, and negatives

_____ School records and/or term papers (yours, not your kids')

_____ Travel souvenirs

_____ Videos and home movies

_____ Wedding stuff

_____ Yearbooks

SAD: Remembrances of poignant milestones, deceased loved ones, personal transitions, and wisdom gained from painful life processes, such as:

_____ Condolence cards and notes

_____ Diaries and journals

_____ Eulogies or programs from memorial services

_____ Keepsakes from departed family members and friends

_____ Obituaries

_____ Pet mementos

GOOD: Stuff that is potentially useful or even monetarily valuable, but otherwise not particularly meaningful, for example:

_____ Artwork, crafts, clothes, or anything you don't use or don't like that were handmade for you or by you

_____ Furnishings you inherited but which don't really suit you

_____ Gifts you never liked

_____ Unappealing heirloom jewelry and trinkets

_____ Your great-uncle's collection of Meerschaum pipes, moose-heads, shells, stamps, or anything else that holds no interest for you

BAD: Reminders of upsetting incidents, unpleasant events, or unfinished business, such as:

_____ Any items from the Happy category list that have the opposite effect on you (list) _____

_____

_____

_____ Broken heirlooms

_____ Negative correspondence ("Dear John" letters, hate mail, bitter divorce-related epistles, etc.)

_____ Hospital souvenirs (ID bracelets, plastic spittoons, jars of kidney stones, etc.)

(M)emorabilia: things remarkable and worthy of remembrance. —*dictionary definition*

Now that you've inventoried your sentimental stuff, I can finally reveal to you my Golden Rule of Memorabilia Management:

Keep only your most special Happy and Sad items; get rid of all Good and Bad ones.

Did you think Good and Happy were a natural pair of "keepers," while Sad and Bad belonged together in the bye-bye bin?

Just like the Good Stuff we dispensed with in Chapter Five, sentimental stuff that's "good" tends to be a major clutter contributor. But because it has a sentimental scent to it, so to speak, it can seem harder to part with. Yet that's precisely why it's so freeing when you do cut the emotional cord. You will feel a wonderful sense of lightness, as though you've been released from bonds you didn't know were binding you.

WHEN THE SENTIMENTAL CLUTTER ISN'T YOURS

As illustrated earlier, it's usually easier to get rid of other people's sentimental stuff than it is to let go of your own. But it's also a mistake to trash anyone else's things without permission, no matter how well you know them or how junky their "clutter" appears to you. If you do this, you're asking for trouble. Your actions, well-meaning as they might be, can be taken as a sign of disrespect. Instead, do whatever you can to involve others in the decluttering decision-making process. If they refuse to either participate or allow you to pitch anything of theirs, and you feel as though the situation has become intolerable, you may need to bring in a neutral third party (e.g., mediator, counselor, organizer). For resources, see Appendix B.

Right about now you may be thinking, "But she doesn't know about *my* stuff—my things are different/valuable/special! Also, my mother/sister/father/brother/aunt/uncle/cousin/best friend would never forgive me if I ever got rid of the (fill in the blank) they gave me." *A reminder:* The choice is yours. Ultimately you will keep whatever you want to keep, so don't waste time justifying your choices or making excuses. Just try to let go of anything you feel ready to shed, and keep moving forward.

● ●
The Gift of Clutter
Just because someone gave it to you doesn't mean you have to keep it forever. Remember the expression, "It's the thought that counts." Treasure the thought behind the gift, but get rid of the gift itself if it doesn't really suit you—unless you don't mind it cluttering up your life.
● ●

Save Only What You Have Space For

If you've shed your negative memorabilia (the Good and Bad stuff), then perhaps you now have sufficient space in which to keep all your positive and poignant mementoes (the Happy and Sad stuff). Or not. Since the Happy category alone contains options for as many types of potential clutter as all the other categories combined, you may still need to do some paring down.

SUPPLIES VERSUS SENTIMENTS

Although shedding sentimental stuff can be more challenging than purging supplies, the process is still applicable. It might be helpful to review Chapter Five's process for deciding how much space to devote to specific kinds of supplies, and how to purge excess by limiting quantity.

Obviously, the amount of space you feel comfortable devoting to storing and/or displaying your memorabilia will dictate how much of it you can keep. (*Reminder:* Mementos, like other forms of stuff, will expand to fill whatever amount of space you allocate for them. So even if you now have sufficient room for everything you've decided to save—watch out!) Saving only the memorabilia you have space for requires making difficult choices. These are choices you'd prefer not to make and that you're probably not used to making. But sometimes we need to shock ourselves into making unfamiliar choices.

When I help clients streamline their memorabilia, I use what I call The Shockers: three tough questions that help shake people out of the sentimental state that they fall into while perusing reminders of the past. These questions can help you during both project and maintenance decluttering (for all types of clutter, not just sentimental stuff).

Shocker 1: What if you had to prepare for a major move?
Oh, what a miserable thought. Go ahead, let yourself dwell on it. Visualize the last time you moved. Was it fun? I doubt it. About the only thing worse than having too much stuff is having to move it. After all, when it comes to moving, a universal truth applies: stuff appears to increase in direct proportion to the dwindling number of days before the movers arrive. (This is especially true when you are moving to a smaller home.)

Remember the sense of panic as moving day crept ever closer? It's true for many people: As time drains away, desperation sets in. A common practice is to finally just stuff all that excess stuff into boxes—some of which remain unpacked for many, many years.

Just as common, however, is the tendency to shed a certain amount of clutter during the moving preparation process. That's why people who move often, such as diplomats and military families, are less likely to accumulate an overabundance of stuff. (As the old saying goes, "A rolling stone gathers no clutter.")

But you don't actually have to be moving in order to move clutter out of your life. Just pretend you're going to move, and see if that doesn't encourage you to let go of more stuff. How? Try adopting a "move mindset." Practice donning mental armor that will help you resist the urge to keep things; visualize it as a protective shield that causes stuff to bounce off instead of sticking to you.

You can fortify yourself by chanting this mantra as you sort and streamline: "The less stuff I choose to keep, the less stuff I have to pack; the less stuff I choose to pack, the less stuff I need to unpack." Imagine you're going to have to pack up and then unpack everything you decide to keep. Visualize yourself performing this drudgery. This can be a very effective clutter-reducing strategy, especially if you have lots of itty-bitty and/or fragile items.

Shocker 2: What if your home was about to catch on fire?
This is even tougher than the thought of packing for a move. The idea of your home going up in flames is almost too awful to contemplate. But that's why this shocker can help you shake loose some more of that clinging clutter.

Imagine that firefighters are struggling to control a blaze next door, and have advised you—the only person home—to leave within 15 minutes since there's a 50-50 chance that your place may catch fire. So, you have exactly 15 minutes to grab your most precious or important things.

(If you have pets, pretend that they've already been moved to safety.) Your car is on the street; fortunately the trunk and seats are empty (good thing you'd already decluttered them!) so there's room for you to load your valuables. Quick—which things will you rescue?

Right now, make a list of every item you can think of that you'd really, truly miss if it went up in flames (or was taken from you in any other way). To jog your memory, you might want to review the checklists of Happy and Sad memorabilia. Use the form on the next page to list not only the stuff itself, but where you would keep each thing so you could locate it quickly.

There are two safe places for keeping precious or important items, and they both have "safe" names: a safe deposit box (often incorrectly called "safety" deposit box); and a fire-resistant safe. The latter option comes in a variety of sizes, shapes, and fire-resistance levels. For example, a file safe, such as the one mentioned in Chapter Four, is designed to hold around a dozen hanging files' worth of documents. You could use it for storing everything from legal and financial records (see Appendix A for a list of which ones you're required to keep) to treasured valentines and diaries. However, it's not designed for storing non-paper items such as slides, negatives, disks, videos, audiotapes, jewelry, or similar meltable objects. Other fire-safe options are available for keeping stuff like that out of harm's way, but they can be quite costly. The safe deposit box may be your best bet for such items.

THE FIRE FANTASY

I've lost count of how many clutter sufferers have said to me, "Sometimes I wish it would all just burn up!" Maybe you've thought that, too. Of course, no one really wants a fire to happen. (I tell people, "Fire is an option—it's just not one I recommend.") But I think that what I call the "fire fantasy" is symbolic of how desperate so many people feel about their clutter-clogged lives. It's not that you really

MY PRECIOUS, IRREPLACEABLE STUFF

Item Description   **Location**

_____   _____

_____   _____

_____   _____

_____   _____

_____   _____

_____   _____

_____   _____

_____   _____

_____   _____

_____   _____

_____   _____

_____   _____

want it to "burn up." You just wish the detritus of delayed decisions and the overflow of opportunities and obligations would simply vanish (like magic, in a puff of smoke!) so you wouldn't have to deal with them.

Of course, most of the things you actually enjoy having around shouldn't be hidden away in safes. They're meant to be displayed, handled, used, read, or looked at ... and appreciated. That's why you want to keep them, right? You can't protect everything you love from every potential hazard; all you can do is take good care of each thing while you've got it and cherish it while you can. And if you try to limit your treasures to what you can take with you in case of an emergency, you'll have more time and space to enjoy them. So remember: If it's not on your list, it probably won't be missed.

PICTURE PERFECT?

Photographs provide a combination of joy and frustration. Some are so important to people that they risk their lives to rescue photo albums from blazing houses. And when other survivors of such catastrophes are interviewed about what objects they most regret losing, photos are usually among the first things mentioned.

Yet the clutter caused by an overabundance of unorganized photos can be a source of stress. There never seems to be enough time to put all your photos into albums. Those hundreds (or thousands) of "wonderful" pictures usually end up languishing in envelopes, baggies, baskets, and/or boxes, just waiting for that proverbial rainy day when you have nothing better to do than deal with them.

Photo clutter may someday become extinct, thanks to all the new computerized camera options. But because there's a huge backlog of existing photos, that day is still a long way off.

If your photo clutter is bothering you, here are the two quickest de-cluttering options:

Photo Storage Boxes.   These are available at many discount de-partment stores and photo processing stores, as well as from catalogs. Each can hold several hundred photos; look for the ones that include sorting dividers and labels.

Get several boxes, schedule some project time, and gather together all your unsorted photos (use a shovel if necessary). If possible, enlist the aid of a discerning family member or friend to help you sort, purge, and organize. Plan to allow time for poring over your pictures; reminiscing about people and events is really the fun part of this process, after all— it's not about efficiency. Just remember to discard any and all photos that you don't like. (For some reason, many people neglect to do this.) Avoid keeping too many duplicates, too. Generally, if you don't send them off to people pretty quickly after you first get them, it's unlikely you'll man-age to get around to it later.

Hire Help.   If you just can't seem to get around to dealing with your photo clutter, then get someone to do it for you. See Appendix B for re-sources.

Shocker 3: What if you were going to die?

This is the toughest one for most of us. We hate to think about our de-mise, especially when there's a lot of clutter involved. (One of my clients put it quite eloquently: "If I died now, and people found out how much clutter I had, I'd just die!")

Think about what you would like to leave behind for your loved ones to deal with. Do you really want them to have to sort through all your clutter after you're gone? (Well, perhaps you do. During one of my work-shops when I'd asked the above question—rhetorically, I'd thought—a wizened woman sitting in the back row spoke up to say, "Aw, it'll serve 'em right!")

Why not toss while you're still the boss? Get rid of excess stuff now. Don't leave behind mess and stress for the grief-stricken. Now is also a good time to make a list of any sentimental items that you would like to leave to specific people or institutions. In the immortal words of either Dear Abby or Ann Landers, "Do your giving while you're living, so you'll be knowing where it's going." (Or something like that.)

Go back to your list of Precious, Irreplaceable Stuff and write in the margin, next to each item, the name of its future recipient. If you change your mind about some of them in the future, you can always revise your list. (That's why erasers and correction fluid were invented.)

SHOCK YOURSELF OUT OF IT

The Shockers are particularly helpful when you start backsliding during any decluttering process. Backsliding is when you gradually find yourself keeping more stuff than you're letting go of—perhaps even going back to "rescue" things from the Donate or Discard bins. When you notice this happening, it's time to take drastic measures. That's what the Shockers are for.

Keep Your Meaningful Mementos
in Simple, Easy-to-Maintain Systems

Back in B.C. times (Before Clutter, that is), our ancestors stored their few precious possessions in a wooden trunk called a hope chest. This was the humble, old-fashioned equivalent of our charming plastic Rubbermaid heavy-duty storage containers. How many of these modern-day hope chests you'll need depends on three factors:

1. How much space you've allocated for your memorabilia museum
2. The types of stuff you've chosen to keep
3. How much stuff you're planning to keep

Of course, you don't have to use plastic storage containers by Rubbermaid (or any other brand, for that matter). If you prefer, you can obtain antique or old-style cedar chests and other kinds of wooden trunks. Other options include archival-quality cardboard boxes—there are even round, hat-box-style units. Or utilize a roll-top desk, a glass-door bookcase, an old dresser, or any article of furniture that's appropriate and available for your purposes.

In fact, most units with drawers work well for storing many types of mementos; it's particularly effective to assign one drawer per category, if possible. For example, a small four-drawer bureau could have one drawer each for old letters and cards (birthday, valentines, holidays, etc.), children's artwork and school papers, photos, and travel souvenirs.

CAPTURE THE IMAGE, LET GO OF THE ITEM

Some sentimental stuff can take up more room than it's worth, especially furnishings, clothes, and various accessories. Take pictures of any items which are simply too bulky to store but which you want to "retain" for posterity; then bid a fond adieu to the actual objects. The only downside is that you may end up adding to your photo clutter.

The key to maintaining any memorabilia management system is to establish an annual or twice-a-year *reminiscence ritual*. This is when you spend at least one afternoon (or whatever part of the day you prefer) to lovingly revisit your sentimental stuff, either alone or with family. Holidays can be a good time to do this, and/or summertime. The purpose of the reminiscence ritual is to allow you to reminisce as you weed out stale mementos, which is a great way to make room for next year's memories. Focus on keeping only the best and most representative items from the past year. If you "can't" seem to let go of enough items, remind yourself that you can keep them all if you really want to, but you'll have to figure out where to store them.

● ●

Stuff to Remember

Designate "memory boxes" or drawers for storing sentimental stuff you choose to keep. Go through the contents periodically. The process should bring up happy memories and also help you weed out anything that is no longer as meaningful. A bonus: it can help cut down on clutter elsewhere, too.

● ●

CHAPTER WRAP-UP

- Save only objects that evoke pleasant or poignant feelings; don't keep anything that makes you feel stressed or upset (unless you are legally required to keep it).
- Decide how much space you can devote to keeping your memorabilia.
- Keep the items that make you feel good in a way that makes you feel good.
- Don't waste time justifying why you want to keep something; if you choose to keep it, decide where you'll store it, and then move on to the next thing.
- Sometimes we need to shock ourselves into making choices that are different from the ones we're used to making.
- Maintain memorabilia management systems by establishing regular "reminiscence rituals" for enjoying your mementos while weeding them to make room for next year's memories.

The Future

· ·

Controlling Your Clutter Quota

Choosing to Be Choosy

● ●

A consequential step in letting go of clutter is learning to use your power of choice to set limits. Why? Because when you don't limit clutter, clutter limits you.

This chapter shows you how to make clutter-conquering choices by becoming more selective. When you know how to choose wisely and well, you can limit your intake of all kinds of potential clutter. Learning how to consistently make effective choices involves several processes:

 TESTING YOUR "YES REFLEX"

2 ABANDONING YOUR ATTITUDE OF ACQUISITION

3 CULTIVATING SELF-TRUST

4 IDENTIFYING YOUR DEFINING ELEMENTS

I got something in the mail recently that made me laugh out loud. It was a department store credit card offer that announced in bold letters on the envelope, "Say YES to MORE of EVERYTHING!" That's exactly what we *don't* need, I thought—more of everything. I tossed it in the recycling bin. But that brazen exhortation to "say YES" got me thinking about how natural it seems for many people to say yes to incoming clutter—instead of choosing to say no.

Has "yes" become a reflex instead of a choice? From what I've observed, the answer is—I hate to say it—yes. And this "yes reflex" is what causes you to become a Clutter Victim.

W ith elaborate consumer profiles on record, consumers come to resemble predictable machines...ready and willing to respond affirmatively when just the right psychological button is pushed. "It's very well known that people are much more susceptible to persuasive appeals when they're distracted," explains University of Texas psychologist Dan Gilbert. "If I'm an advertiser, I want you to be under information (over)load in as many circumstances as possible."
—*From "Data Smog" by David Shenk*

VICTIMS OF CLUTTER

By allowing yourself to become conditioned to automatically say yes to the onrushing river of offers, information, "free gifts," rebates, deals, steals, and stuff of all kinds, you turn yourself into a Clutter Victim. Think about what a victim is: someone who doesn't have a choice. So when you voluntarily (though unconsciously) give away your power of choice, you become a victim. Every time you claim you can't say no to or can't let go of a clutter-causing offer or object, you are reinforcing your victimhood... and letting these "clutter culprits" grip you ever tighter.

Victim of Clutter

That's why I say the most important piece of clutter to let go of is the apostrophe *t* on the end of *can't*. When I catch clients saying, "I can't get rid of this," I tell them, "Yes, you can. If I held a gun to your head, you could get rid of that piece of clutter right now. You're just not choosing to get rid of it—yet." Then I have them rephrase the original statement; they must say instead, "I'm choosing to keep this piece of clutter" (or, "I'm choosing to let go of it"—when they're ready to).

What happens when you admit that you're actually making a choice? You are leaving the door open to other choices. This means you can start making different choices. For example, you *can* get rid of that piece of clutter whenever you want to. You are no longer a Clutter Victim when you reclaim your power of choice.

WHY *CAN'T* YOU?

Practice being conscious of how often you claim you "can't" say no to or let go of something. When you catch yourself doing it, change

"I can't" to "I'm choosing not to"—or to "I can." Remember, *can't* is a cop-out; using that word is just a way of not taking responsibility for your choices.

FEAR OF NO

But what if you're afraid to say no ... afraid you'll miss out on something worthwhile ... afraid you'll lose out on a valuable opportunity to save money, or get something for nothing, or, or ...

Let's look at what you're really afraid of.

In terms of creating clutter, the fear of not getting something and regretting it is identical to the fear of getting rid of something and regretting it. (Review Chapter One for suggestions and exercises on overcoming fear of regret.) So both forms of fear-of-regret tend to generate enormous amounts of clutter.

Consider the most common clutter-friendly offers in the accompanying checklist. I call them opportunities disguised as obligations, because they are all designed to make you feel obligated to "take advantage" of them. But what if it is actually *you* who is being taken advantage of? Offers are created to extract something valuable from you. This is usually money and data (in the form of your buying habits); your time, space, and/or energy are extracted too, but those may not be valuable commodities to anyone but you.

● ●
Offers are always carefully worded to prey upon your fears of "missing out" or "losing out."
● ●

If you are like most people in this country, you will have checked off at least 6 of the 12 types of offers listed. Now you may be feeling defen-

TEST YOUR "YES" REFLEX

Put a checkmark (✓) by any of the opportunities disguised as obligations that you are in the habit of saying yes to. Blanks are provided for additional options.

_____ airline mileage programs

_____ "frequent buyer" programs

_____ credit cards that offer you "points" for airline mileage and frequent buyer programs

_____ supermarket "savings clubs" and "rewards programs"

_____ department store and mall shopping programs

_____ grocery and other store coupons

_____ restaurant 2-for-1 coupons

_____ coupons for services (car and household repairs and maintenance)

_____ rebates (mail-in)

_____ "free" gift-with-purchase offers (including publication subscriptions)

_____ "buy one, get one free" offers (or similar "quantity discounts")

_____ sweepstakes-style contests

_____ _____

_____ _____

_____ _____

_____ _____

sive, perhaps even outraged, by the implication that you should be saying anything other than a resounding *yes* to them. You're not alone, either. Here are some of the most common defenses that my clients and students routinely bring up:

"I save hundreds of dollars every year using grocery coupons."

"I get free airfare for my vacations, thanks to my frequent flier miles."

"Without 2-for-1 coupons, we might never eat out at nice restaurants."

"My favorite department store sends me a $20 gift certificate every time I accumulate enough points on my credit card."

"I had to join my supermarket's shopping club to get the discount prices on the groceries I buy regularly."

These are all valid defenses, and I can personally relate to several of them. By no means am I suggesting that you should say no to *all* offers. What I'm advising against, however, is automatically saying yes without considering the potential clutter consequences. (Did you happen to notice a correlation between any items you checked off and the clutter that regularly accumulates on your kitchen table or counter space?)

This "yes habit" is a tough one to break, because so many offers do seem really worthwhile. Some offers actually are worthwhile; it just depends on whether they're really worth *your* while. How can you tell the difference between which ones are and which aren't? Look over the Yes Reflex checklist and think about how each offer you checked affects your life. Do the benefits consistently outweigh the drawbacks—or vice versa? Specifically, do you find it easy to maintain the programs and utilize the rewards, or do you ever feel overwhelmed and overburdened by the sense that you "should" be keeping better track of all this stuff? For example:

- Participating in various programs often entails having to keep track of points earned in order to make sure you're not being "cheated" out of your proper rewards. Moreover, if you don't regularly keep track of those monthly statements, both paper clutter and stress levels tend to rise. You also need to keep an eye on deadlines and expiration dates so you don't "waste" your accumulated miles, points, etc. And don't forget the time and paper and decision making involved in choosing how to "spend" all those miles and points.

- Rebate offers need to be mailed in by a deadline date, and you have to remember to include the UPC code and get a photocopy made of the receipt to go with the completed form. Then it's wise to mark your calendar for 90 days later in case you don't receive your rebate check (a common problem) and need to follow up. Of course, you'll also need a file or other good place to keep a copy of the paperwork.

- Coupons usually have expiration dates. This gives you something else to keep track of, therefore requiring a coupon-organizing system. (As for the coupons that don't have an expiration date, one client explained to me, "If it doesn't have an expiration date, that means you can never throw it out.")

CONQUERING COUPON CLUTTER

If you're going to clip coupons, you might as well do it in a way that doesn't create clutter and chaos for you. The following steps can help transform your couponing from a stressful, clutter-producing chore into a fun and profitable process.

SEVEN STEPS FOR SUCCESSFUL COUPONING

1. Establish a positive attitude: Think of couponing as a profitable hobby.

2. Set aside sufficient time on at least a weekly basis to clip and sort coupons in a leisurely fashion.

3. To make your couponing ritual pleasant and efficient, make sure you have the following: (a) a comfortable chair; (b) adequate lighting; (c) an uncluttered, spacious surface on which to put the coupons (laps don't count!).

4. Sort coupons into your coupon organizer either immediately as you clip them, or at the end of each "coupon session." (If yours is the latter style, then at least sort coupons into Food and Nonfood stacks as you go along; this will save you time later.) Avoid leaving a pile of coupons to be sorted later, because procrastination often means clutter.

5. If you clip a coupon you'd like to use on your next shopping trip, the following two steps are recommended: (a) Write a *C* next to each item on your shopping list for which you have a coupon. (b) Slip the coupon into the Today's Purchases slot in your coupon organizer.

6. Bring your coupon organizer with you anytime you shop.

7. Periodically (monthly) weed through your coupon organizer to discard expired coupons and note coupons with upcoming expiration dates. Move these to your Today's Purchases section and note on your shopping list.

Do not become obsessive about using *all* coupons before they expire. If you occasionally miss a coupon deadline, so what? There will always be more coupons!

● ●
When Expired Is Desired
Why does finding an expired coupon often provoke a reaction of relief rather than one of dismay? Because time has made the decision for you!
● ●

CHOOSE AN ANTI-CLUTTER ATTITUDE

How can you learn to consistently make choices that will keep you from cluttering up your life? First, work on abandoning your attitude of acquisition.

It's important to understand that there are two main things you can change about yourself that will help you let go of clutter: your attitude and your habits. Neither is easy to change, but of the two changing your attitude is most essential. Change your clutter-attracting attitude, and you won't have to change as many habits. When you realize you don't need to acquire many of the things that continually clutter your life, you'll have less stuff to shuffle, sort, organize, store, take care of, keep track of, repair, maintain—all of which require not just time, but "good habits."

Clutter is, at bottom, mainly about attitude. To be free of "stuff stress," you need to let go of either the attitude that causes you to acquire clutter or the attitude that makes you feel bad about keeping it. (If you must keep hanging on to stuff, accept it, and stop torturing yourself about it already!) Letting go of clutter is not just about getting rid of stuff; it's also about resisting the urge to acquire and accumulate. Look at it this way. If you follow the advice from Chapter Five about getting rid of one unit of clutter each day, but you keep taking in at least two units of clutter a day, you're not going to be seeing results anytime soon.

Get in the habit of consciously choosing to limit your intake of potential clutter. Learning to set limits is a crucial part of this process. Start setting limits by practicing saying no to things, offers, activities, and people that use up your money, time, efforts, and energy in unfulfilling ways. The word *no* has been called the most powerful time management tool ever invented. So work on saying no to incoming clutter of all kinds on a daily basis, and you can start saying yes to whatever you'd really rather spend your resources on.

Here's how to get in the habit of choosing to limit your clutter quota. Unless you are a hermit, you'll probably have several opportunities each day to practice using these steps. Remember, you have nothing to lose, except clutter.

"Today more of us in America than anywhere else in the world have the luxury of choice between simplicity and complication of life. And for the most part, we, who could choose simplicity, choose complication."
—*Anne Morrow Lindbergh, in* Gift from the Sea *(1955)*

Six Steps to Making Clutter-Conquering Choices

1. BE AWARE. Be aware of each opportunity to make a choice as it presents itself. Be aware means "beware"; clutter possibilities may lurk behind even the most innocent-seeming offers and requests. Keep a copy of your Yes Reflex checklist handy, and feel free to make additions to it as new options arise.

2. QUESTION. Question the value of things that are presented to you as "free," "important," "valuable," or any other highly subjective terms. For example, is it really free if it costs you time or energy? How important is it, exactly? What is the real value of a supposedly valuable offer or object? Ask yourself: "If I had never learned of this offer, would I be OK?"

3. WAIT. Don't let yourself be rushed into making a decision; most choices can wait. Use this Samurai philosophy: "Refrain until you can respond instead of react." For example, when faced with a "Special Deal—Buy Now and Save!" offer for something you don't urgently need, instead of reacting with "I'd better get this now in case the price goes up," you might tell yourself, "I'll wait to get this because the price may go down."

4. ACKNOWLEDGE. Acknowledge that you are making a conscious choice by saying, "I am choosing to ..." You are more powerful when you choose than when you allow circumstances or others to choose for you. Reinforce your power by remind-

ing yourself that you are capable of making effective choices, and acknowledge yourself for all the times you have chosen well.

5. **FOLLOW INSTINCT.** Pay attention to your instincts; gut feelings are invariably worth following. Let your inner voice help you choose what's best for you. The more you practice being instinctive, the better you'll get at hearing that inner voice.

6. **TRUST.** Trust that you have made the best possible choice for any given moment; let go of the choice and move on. Trust is what enables you to part with past choices instead of mourning the road not taken, allowing you to keep moving forward with confidence. It frees you from endlessly second-guessing yourself with "what-ifs" and torturing your mind with "shoulda's."

Of the six steps in the process of making clutter-conquering choices, trust is perhaps the most important—and it is the hardest to practice. It's useful to look at the reasons behind this.

I've observed that the majority of people who don't have clutter seem to trust themselves to make good choices, while most people who struggle with clutter tend to *hope* they're making good choices. It's human nature to be hopeful, and hope can help get you through tough times. But the problem with hope is that it leaves room for uncertainty and indecision, which hold the door wide open for clutter to come marching in. Clutter asks, "What if you get rid of this and then find out you need it?" Uncertainty replies, "I guess I should keep it." Clutter exhorts, "What if you don't take advantage of this offer and you miss out on a fabulous deal?" Indecision responds, "Maybe I should think about this later; I'll just set it aside for now."

Trust is what lets you answer "So what!" to those questions, and to say "Go away!" when clutter comes knocking. When you trust that you'll always be able to make the best of the outcome of your choices, you can enjoy the present and look toward the future without getting mired in the past. You don't have to hope that things will turn out OK because you *know* they will. How do you know? Because you give yourself credit for being a resourceful and resilient person. After all, you've managed to get this far in life somehow. You've probably overcome a variety of obstacles, setbacks, perhaps even outright disasters or tragedies, and you're still here.

Perhaps you're thinking: "But I've made some pretty bad choices in my life." It's OK. Most of us have made bad choices along the way. That's not the point. Until time travel is perfected, we can't go back and do anything about our past choices. But what you can change are your future choices. So starting today, practice making a conscious effort to trust yourself to choose more wisely.

HOW TO BE SUCCESSFULLY SELECTIVE

How can you trust yourself to make effective clutter-limiting choices when you have a history of being a clutter magnet? The answer can be found by examining the things you've acquired that aren't clutter: the objects that you like and actually use; the stuff that makes your life easier or more enjoyable. By identifying what I call the *defining elements* of anything that works for you, you are able to become more selective and, therefore, make better choices.

Take clothes, for instance. If you have the common complaint of "too many clothes but nothing to wear," go to your closet (or wherever you keep your apparel) and pull out only the items you actually wear regularly and on special occasions. What are the specific elements they all have in common that make you reach for them again and again? It's time to figure out precisely *why* you seem to feel so comfortable and/or good in these clothes, so that when you shop for new items you can avoid choosing things that lack the defining elements you require. Knowing those elements helps you edit your options and ultimately make choices you'll be happy with.

"Elegance is refusal." —*Diana Vreeland*

I'll share one of my defining elements with you, just to give you an idea of how this technique works. Years ago, I decided to pay attention to the clothing features that really worked for me. One of the things I noticed was that I avoided wearing any outfit that lacked pockets, even if I liked everything else about it—color, fit, fabric, style, etc. Pockets turned out to be a key defining element for me. Now when I shop (which I rarely do), I won't even consider trying on any item without pockets because I already know I'd never wear it. And since many articles of women's apparel don't have real pockets—although some, strangely, have "faux" ones—my *choice field* is automatically limited.

Identifying this one defining element started saving me time, money and, of course, clutter. Over the years, I have refined my defining elements for the pockets themselves, so that now, not just any pocket will do. I've actually evolved to a state of pocket pickiness that only permits me to consider garments with certain kinds of pockets that fit my exacting criteria. And, by the way, pockets are only one of dozens of defining elements that I've identified for myself.

By continuing to refine and edit each of your defining elements, you keep reducing the potential for acquiring stuff. The longer your list of criteria, the pickier you are—and the less clutter you'll have.

The accompanying worksheet is designed to help you figure out your own defining elements for all your major clutter-causing stuff. Keep the best and let go of the rest. Here's how to do it.

Instructions for the Defining Elements Worksheet

1. Plan to spend approximately 90 minutes on this exercise.
2. Review your Clutter Categories Checklist from Chapter Two to remind yourself of the specific types of things that generate the most clutter for you in the categories of Supplies, Household, and Clothing and Accessories.
3. In the left-hand column of the worksheet, list the top five types of clutter-causing items from those categories (e.g., apparel, shoes, linens/towels, gift wrap/ribbons, videos).
4. Go and pick out your absolute favorite from each of those five types of things. Favorites are the things you use most often, or

they are the ones you like so much, you only use them sparingly so they won't get "used up."

5. One at a time, focus on each favorite and try to identify why you like it so much: What are its defining elements—the specific features that make it work so well for you and that you would like all other items of its type to have? (See the sample completed worksheet for ideas.) Then list these elements in the right-hand column. Be as detailed as possible. If you run out of room, use another page.

6. Use your defining elements to help you be highly selective when shopping for replacement items and as criteria for choosing which objects to keep or let go of. (Get rid of all items that lack any of the defining elements for that item type.)

7. Make a conscious effort to notice the defining elements of any other types of items you'd like to be more selective about.

SAMPLE DEFINING ELEMENTS

These examples are not meant to be used as models. They are just samples to show you how the process works.

Type of Item	Defining Elements
1. slacks, skirts, suits	pockets, no belt loops; solid jewel-tone colors, no light colors; wool blend or cotton, knits or twill
2. shoes	maximum 2-inch heel, no spikes; smooth leather, not suede; good arch support, must be comfortable
3. linens/towels	250-thread-count minimum; white or light color, no patterns; all-cotton, no synthetics
4. gift wrap/ ribbons	all-occasion, no special-occasion designs; gift-bags or flat wrap, not rolls; iridescent/transparent, not opaque
5. videos	under 2 hours; comedy, romantic comedy, classics; foreign with subtitles, not dubbed

DEFINING ELEMENTS WORKSHEET

Type of Item	Defining Elements
1. _____	_____
	_____
	_____
	_____
	_____
2. _____	_____
	_____
	_____
	_____
	_____
3. _____	_____
	_____
	_____
	_____
4. _____	_____
	_____
	_____
5. _____	_____
	_____
	_____
	_____
	_____

HONING YOUR "REJECT REFLEX"

Ever wondered why you don't wear something even though it's your "best" color or your favorite fabric? The problem may be that the item doesn't include a sufficient number of your defining elements.

Often closets are cluttered with clothes that were purchased for one or more of the following seemingly good reasons:

- On sale
- Nice color
- Good fabric
- Fits well
- Designer label

Once you've identified and refined your defining elements, you'll be less likely to make the mistake of buying things for any of those reasons. Knowing the combination of specific criteria you need in order to make a purchase helps turn your Yes Reflex into a Reject Reflex.

Become a connoisseur of yourself: by studying which things work best for you, you'll learn how to avoid acquiring potential clutter.

BE PICKY . . . AND PROUD OF IT

The more choosy you become, the less clutter you'll acquire. Practice rejecting it before it can get close enough to stick to you. Don't let it come through your door. Remember, being choosy, selective, discerning, or (as some may call you) picky is one of the best ways to shut off your clutter-attraction switch.

Becoming choosy forces you to redefine what it means to *waste* something. Like the words *can't, should, free,* and *valuable, waste* is a clutter-attracting word which, when left unchallenged, can be dangerous. The "don't-waste-it syndrome" causes way too much clutter to accumulate. Question why turning your home into a dump is less wasteful than taking your clutter to the dump. It's the same reasoning that says you should finish everything on your plate although you're stuffed, because discarding any food that's left would be "wasting" it. (Even as a child I found this reasoning illogical.)

Just as picky eaters rarely become overweight, picky consumers rarely become overstuffed. So use your power of choice as an anti-stuff shield.

> "He who knows that enough is enough will always have enough." —*Lao Tzu*

THE RIVER OF NO RETURN

Visualize an endless, flowing river. Imagine that it's composed of an infinite amount of information, opportunities, and objects. Picture yourself dipping into this river whenever you choose to, at your own pace, anytime you feel thirsty. You'll use a teaspoon, a glass, or a cup, but not a bucket—after all, you're not trying to bail it out. That would be impossible.

Know that this river will never run dry, so you can relax. You're not going to "miss" anything; there will always be more stuff flowing by. And no one else will ever get ahead of it or catch up with it, either.

You won't drown in this river. You're safe. Let it flow, and let it go.

CHAPTER WRAP-UP

- The most important piece of clutter to let go of is the apostrophe *t* on the end of *can't*.

- Stop automatically saying yes to offers that are opportunities disguised as obligations.
- There are two main things you can change about yourself that will help you let go of clutter: your attitude and your habits. Of the two, attitude is the most essential.
- An attitude of self-trust is an invaluable aid to staying uncluttered.
- Giving yourself credit for being resourceful and resilient can help you stop being a Clutter Victim.

Managing Mental Clutter

• •

A significant step in letting go of clutter involves learning how to stop overloading your mind and memory. Why? Because an uncluttered mind is key to an uncluttered life.

OVERVIEW

This chapter presents specific tools for helping you deal with most of the stuff that clutters up your mind: to-do's, information, worries, and grievances. Mental clutter is intangible, but it often contributes to tangible clutter—and vice versa. There are two main sources of mental clutter:

 STUFF TO REMEMBER

2 STUFF TO FORGET

During one of my Letting Go of Clutter workshops, I was in the middle of a discussion about to-do lists when a white-haired woman spoke up. "I have discovered the secret to achieving peace of mind," she announced boldly. Everyone in the room turned to look at her expectantly, including me. (I was hoping she wasn't going to start talking about a spaceship voyage.)

"Please, tell us what it is," I asked politely.

"Well," she said, "I'm eighty years old and I still seem to have too many to-do's to do. So now, any time I think of something else I ought to do but probably won't get around to in this lifetime...I just put it on my Next-Life List."

I had to admit it was a great idea—especially since it didn't involve extraterrestrials.

I can't promise that using a Next-Life List will help you achieve peace of mind, but it just might. Creating different kinds of lists can be an effective way to manage all the stuff that clogs your mind by crowding your memory and clouding your judgment.

Before we get into the fine art of list-making, though, it's helpful to gain a basic understanding of the sources and symptoms of mental clutter.

FROM INTANGIBLE TO TANGIBLE, AND VICE VERSA

There are two main contributors to mental clutter:

- Stuff to remember—to-do's and information
- Stuff to forget—worries and grievances

Although seemingly intangible, both sources of mental clutter can influence you to accumulate the more concrete kinds of clutter covered earlier. Mental clutter may cause you to:

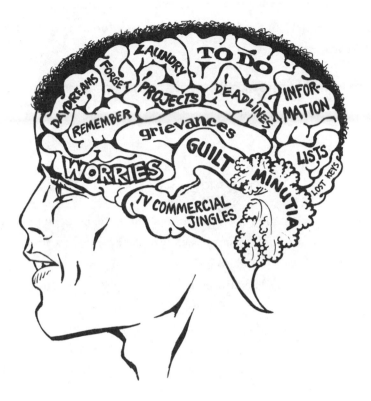

MENTAL CLUTTER: The two main contributors to mental clutter—
Stuff to Remember and Stuff to Forget

- Forget where you put things, so you end up purchasing more of what you know you have "somewhere"
- Feel too overwhelmed to make decisions, so you find yourself surrounded by piles of paper and objects
- Have trouble focusing, so you keep getting sidetracked
- Be plagued with a pervasive, uneasy feeling that you've forgotten something you were supposed to do

Of course, it's also possible that your tangible clutter is contributing to your mental clutter. Like the chicken-or-egg question, it's hard to say which comes first, but either way it can make for a vicious clutter-to-clutter cycle.

"Disposal is the handmaiden of an orderly mind."
—*Norm Crampton*

LIBERATED BY LISTS

Effective list-making may help you break that cycle by giving you a way to declutter your mind. A list is basically a place for you to dump out the stuff that's "on your mind" so it doesn't get overloaded.

Few of us nowadays are able to rely solely on our minds to remember everything we need or want to recall. Even if we could remember everything, what would be the point of wasting so many brain cells on mundane stuff? After all, even Albert Einstein supposedly refused to memorize his own phone number because he said he knew where he could look it up. (I'll bet he'd just ask his wife. But that's not the point.) Yet many people do inadvertently and unnecessarily overburden their brains, leaving insufficient "mind space" for reflection and creative problem solving.

Making lists can help you manage the mental clutter caused by stuff to remember and stuff to forget. List-making is a mind-decluttering process; the actual lists—the product of the process—are life-management tools.

Each of the following types of lists is useful for a different aspect of mental decluttering:

- Master lists
- Step-by-step lists
- Maintenance checklists
- Un-to-do lists

- Information lists
- Pros & cons lists
- Grievance lists
- Emergency mini-lists

MASTER LISTS

Complaining about to-do lists is a popular pastime. I understand why. You see, in my line of work I get to look at a lot of to-do lists because my clients often ask me for advice on how to do their to-do's. I've noticed a common flaw in the way most of these lists are composed.

The typical to-do list tends to include a variety of unrelated reminders, such as:

1. Write thank-yous.
2. Reorganize filing system.
3. Clean out garage.

Number 4 might as well be: Become a neurosurgeon.

The main thing these four items have in common is that they're all described in just three words. This conciseness serves a purpose: it makes it easy to move big projects from list to list, forever—which is exactly what usually happens because they rarely get done. And that's the key reason so many people complain about their to-do lists.

If you're tired of moving your reminders from list to list, I recommend using a categorized Master List so you stop lumping all your unrelated projects and tasks together. The Master List Form provided here may help you get started, or you can create your own customized version if you prefer. The point is to get in the habit of grouping all similar to-do's, which makes it easier to see which ones are maintenance-related and which are projects.

MASTER LIST FORM

Calls

Correspondence/To Send

Projects/To Do

Errands/To Go

To Order/To Obtain

Miscellaneous

STEP-BY-STEP LISTS

Your next step is to break down projects, such as "reorganize filing system" and "clean out garage," into smaller steps. (By the way, if you really are planning to reorganize your filing system, those steps are provided in Chapter Four; and Chapter Five includes the steps for garage decluttering.) It's like that old riddle—Question: How do you eat an elephant? Answer: One bite at a time. Breaking down your larger to-do's into bite-sized pieces will make almost any project more doable.

Unfortunately, this step-by-step listing process usually involves taking the time to think projects through from beginning to end, which is something most people prefer not to do. (As Thomas Alva Edison once wrote, "There is no expedient to which a man will not go to avoid the real labor of thinking.") But it's what you have to do if you want to see the results and feel the sense of accomplishment instead of just moving stuff from list to list.

● ●

Another option: declutter your to-do list by deciding which projects you don't really have to do, and removing them.

● ●

After you finish listing the steps, pencil in a time estimate next to each task or project step. If you have trouble coming up with time estimates, use "two hours" as a step starting point; you can always change it later (that's the point of using pencil). The main thing is to get yourself in the habit of thinking how much time you need to schedule in order to get your to-do's done. Doing this with all your to-do's will make your lists work better for you. And since the purpose of lists is to help declutter your mind by supporting your memory, this is advice worth remembering.

"(T) ime given to thought is the greatest time-saver of all." —*Norman Cousins*

MAINTENANCE CHECKLISTS

As you learned earlier, life is 90 percent maintenance, which means there are far too many ongoing, mundane maintenance tasks for you to remember. (If you need a reminder of why this is true, go take another look at the Maintenance Checklist in Chapter Three.) Yet it's a Catch-22 kind of thing: all those tasks need to be done too often to keep noting them on to-do lists or in your time management system; but because they're not on your lists, you're forever juggling forgot-to-do's. This creates an ideal incubator for growing mental clutter.

Typical real-life examples: Perhaps you intend to take your vitamins every day, but you forget to do that almost as often as you remember. Or maybe you're supposed to water certain houseplants frequently, but they keep dying because you don't remember to do this consistently. These types of memory lapses can be both sources and symptoms of mental clutter. They create the equivalent of running a constant low-grade fever, because they undermine your sense of well-being by giving you an ongoing, nagging sense of having forgotten something you "know" you're supposed to do.

That's why I recommend creating your own customized Maintenance Checklists. Start by making a list of the types of things you often forget to do. If you can't remember what those are, review Chapter Three's Maintenance Checklist for clues. So you'll see that nothing is too mundane to be on your personalized checklists, here's some of the things on mine:

_____ Make bed

_____ Do eye exercises

_____ Take vitamins

_____ Walk/exercise

_____ Water plants

_____ Empty wastebaskets

_____ Floss

You might call it obsessive, petty, ridiculous or whatever you want, but the results are worth it: using checklists ensures that your mind will almost never be cluttered with little voices saying, "You forgot something" (a form of clutter-mutter which many people have told me they deal with daily).

Don't make the mistake of thinking that tools like this will weaken your memory, or that "smart people" should be able to remember stuff without assistance. Checklists help support your mind by keeping it free for thinking instead of cluttered with things to remember. (Think of Einstein.)

"The true art of memory is the art of attention."
—*Samuel Johnson*

SANITY SAVER

It's happened again. You just can't seem to remember where you put something that was in your hand a mere moment ago. And you haven't been able to find it despite a frenzied search. But I'll bet I know where it is: underneath something—a larger object that you absent-mindedly placed on top of it.

Tip: Never—even for a second—put a bigger thing, such as a newspaper or a jacket, on top of a smaller thing, such as keys or glasses.

LARGER OBJECTS	that typically hide these	SMALLER OBJECTS
newspaper or magazine	hides	glasses or scissors
jacket or sweater	hides	keys or wallet
notebook or binder	hides	disk or calculator

Resolve to make an ongoing effort to be conscious of what you do. There's no substitute for paying attention.

UN TO DO LISTS

As my student with the "Next-Life List" understood so well, there's always going to be more to do than any of us will ever get done. Giving yourself permission to list things you know you may never get around to doing can help you shed more mental clutter. When you jot down any potential project that pops into your head, the process releases you from feeling any need to hold onto the idea. (By the way, it's good to note the date anytime you record your ideas, so when you review your list it gives you a sense of history.) Whether you call it a Next-Life List or, as I do, an "Un-To-Do List," the mental decluttering effect is the same. Sometimes just getting it out of your head is a way to let go of excess stuff.

● ●
To-Do or Un-To-Do, That Is the Question
If you end up deciding that an un-to-do project is actually worth doing, you can always transfer it to your master list—and vice versa.
● ●

INFORMATION LISTS

The more we are bombarded with information, the less capable we become of storing it in our ever-dwindling memory cells. Trying to remember too many phone numbers, addresses, bank account numbers, etc., can overburden the brain with information that could easily be stored elsewhere. (Again, remember Einstein.)

"Elsewhere" can be as simple as condensing your most important info onto a one-page list. Then you can reduce the list on a copier to the size of an index card (or at least a half-sheet) that can fit in your wallet.

Take some time—perhaps an hour—to choose and assemble the information you want to include on this list. (Ideally, you can use a computer so you'll be able to update the information easily.) You might also want to keep an extra copy in your fire-resistant file safe.

PROS & CONS LISTS

While the previous types of lists deal with managing to-do's and information, the pros & cons list is unique because it's designed for managing a different source of clutter: worry. Worrying produces noxious clouds of mental clutter that can make it difficult to see solutions and stay on track. (And worrying about your clutter is very efficient—you're simultaneously cluttering with tangibles and intangibles.)

The pros & cons list method was originally described by Benjamin Franklin in 1772. In a letter responding to someone who had requested advice on how to solve problems without worrying, Franklin explained the way this list-making process works:

> ...My way is to divide half a sheet of paper by a line into two columns; writing over the one *Pro,* and over the other *Con.* Then during three or four days' consideration I put down under the different heads short hints of the different motives that at different times occur to me, *for* or *against* the measure. When I have thus got them all together in one view, I endeavour to estimate their respective weights; and where I find two (one on each side) that seem equal, I strike them both out. If I find a reason *pro* equal to some two reasons *con,* I strike out the three. If I judge some

two reasons *con* equal to some three reasons *pro,* I strike out the five; and thus proceeding I find out where the balance lies.

This exercise is effective because it gets you to organize your thoughts so clearly and compactly, there's no place left for worry. Franklin observed:

> When...difficult cases occur, they are difficult chiefly because while we have them under consideration, all the reasons *pro* and *con* are not present to the mind at the same time.... Hence the various purposes or inclinations that alternately prevail, and the uncertainty that perplexes us.

All in all, a pretty accurate description of the mental clutter caused by worry. Some things never change. Which is why the pros & cons list method is still valid. Try it the next time you catch yourself worrying, and you'll see how well it works.

"When I look back on all these worries, I remember the story of the old man who said on his deathbed that he had had a lot of trouble in his life, most of which never happened."
—*Winston Churchill*

HOW TO TAKE A LOAD OFF YOUR MIND

Perhaps making pros & cons lists seems like too much trouble. Or maybe you feel this technique just doesn't apply to your particular worries. If so, consider simply jotting down either a list or a description of whatever concerns are cluttering up your mind. The therapeutic benefits of putting thoughts on paper have actually been scientifically documented.

According to a piece in *Newsweek* magazine, studies have shown that "cathartic writing" can lower blood pressure and increase the level of disease-fighting lymphocytes in the bloodstream. The article notes that "Even the best-adjusted and healthiest people acquire emotional baggage in the course of a lifetime—be it...conflicts with friends and family or remorse over missteps and lost opportunities." It goes on to say that writing about our concerns "forces us to transform the ruminations cluttering up our minds into coherent stories."

GRIEVANCE LISTS

Next to worrying, holding onto grievances is an excellent way to clutter up your mind. If you have trouble letting go of insults, injustices, and instances of ingratitude, you might be carrying around a lot of excess baggage you're not even aware of.

To lighten your load, make a list of all your grievances (along with the perpetrators' names, of course). Downloading this type of stuff from your brain onto a page can create more room on your mental hard drive; it also may be somewhat therapeutic. See, you don't have to forgive if you're not ready to, but perhaps you can forget (especially once you've got it all recorded for posterity).

"There's worse things than having a bad memory—like remembering stuff that should have been forgotten long ago." *—Anonymous*

EMERGENCY MINI-LISTS

When your brain starts feeling overloaded, it can trigger an attack of "overwhelm." If you sense one coming on, sit down and take a few deep breaths (remember to exhale, too). Then quickly make a brief list of whatever you absolutely must get done within the next hour. Focus only on your most immediate must-do's. This will help you declutter your mind and gain some sense of control.

WHAT ABOUT LIST CLUTTER?

Maybe you're thinking. "Don't all these lists create more clutter?" Well, they can if you let them. But you don't have to let them. Set up a "Lists and Checklists" hanging file (as shown in Chapter Four's Sample File Chart). Divide the contents with folders labeled for blank checklist forms and old lists, if you choose to retain some for reference or record keeping. (You'll need to weed and/or archive the latter folder regularly to prevent it from getting huge.)

CHAPTER WRAP-UP

- Intangible clutter can cause you to attract tangible clutter—and vice versa.
- List-making is both a process and a tool for dealing with the different types of mental clutter.
- Describing major projects in just three words makes it easy to keep moving them from list to list; but to get them off your lists, you need to break them down into step-by-step tasks first.
- Never put a bigger object on top of a smaller item, even for a second.
- If you can't forgive, at least forget; it will reduce your load of mental clutter.

Afterword: More Top Clutter Questions and Answers

● ●

I hope this book has already given you all the methods and motivation you'll ever need to help you let go of clutter. But just in case you're still looking for a few more decluttering tips, tools, and techniques, here are some runners-up to the Top 10 Clutter Questions, along with my answers.

If you should ever have any questions or suggestions about conquering clutter, please contact me via my online advice column at www.MiracleOrganizing.com, or write to me care of The Miracle Worker Organizing Service, PMB 199, 3368 Governor Drive, San Diego, CA 92122.

Books

Q: I have boxes and boxes of books in the garage—no place to store them, yet I feel reluctant to get rid of them. What can I do?

A: Books are tangible manifestations of what we would like to think is our knowledge. That's a key reason why it's so difficult for many of us to let go of them. But difficult does not equal impossible when you follow these steps:

    1. Decide how much room and which areas you are comfortable devoting to book storage.

    2. Get shelves that are designed for books, not stereo equipment or knickknacks. If shelves are too deep you'll end up stacking

stuff in front of the books; too much space between shelves makes it easy to layer other clutter on top of the books.

3. Compare the amount of books you have with the space you've allocated for book storage; then calculate the discrepancy between the two in terms of the approximate number of books you need to eliminate.

4. With that goal in mind, begin weeding (not reading!) and don't stop until you've hit the goal number. (Note: Chapters Four and Five offer applicable weeding advice.)

5. For maintenance, get in the habit of utilizing your local library in two ways: (a) donate excess books for book sales; (b) borrow books and magazines. Buy only those books that you either can't get from the library or that you decide you want to own after borrowing them. Also, remember to use the In-Out Inventory Rule. (See Chapter Five for details.)

"Bookshelves need as much weeding as a garden and the weeds are not so apparent."   —*Andy Rooney*

Instructions and Warranties

Q: What can I do with all these instruction pamphlets and warranties I keep stuffing in my kitchen drawers?

A: First, weed out the ones that are no longer relevant or valid. (Use the purging processes described in Chapter Four.) I've noticed that, on average, almost 50 percent of this type of clutter consists of outdated materials; for example, manuals relating to products you don't even own anymore and warranties that expired long ago.

Once you've purged, you're ready to organize what's left. Instructions and warranties come in a variety of shapes, sizes, and thicknesses, and therefore can be awkward to file. I recommend

Recipe for Clutter

storing them in loose-leaf binders with top-loading plastic sheet protectors and tabbed dividers. Some instruction pamphlets come already hole-punched; the sheet protectors only need to be used for the odd-sized ones as well as for the warranties and related receipts. The dividers can be labeled by category or area (e.g., kitchen, garage, home office).

Recipes

Q: What do I do with stacks, drawers, and boxes full of recipes I've collected for years (I have hundreds of them)?

A: Sounds like you've got a recipe for "stuffed papers." You can get that off the back burner by first figuring out your defining elements for recipes (see Chapter Seven for this process). For example, one of my own "recipe rules" is that I save only those that require five ingredients or less. (Obviously, I have no intention of ever becoming a gourmet cook.) This automatically eliminates about 90 percent of the recipes I come across.

Once you've established your criteria for keeping recipes, decide how much space and which area you'll devote to storing them. Unless you're only saving recipes for reading instead of cooking, the kitchen is a likely candidate; a counter near the stove is often most convenient.

Like instructions and warranties, recipes can be stored quite effectively in loose-leaf binders with clear plastic, top-loading sheet protectors. Since sheet protectors wipe clean, the recipes you actually use will remain unsullied by the usual clinging globs and splatters of cooking ingredients. And because they're clear, they eliminate the need to recopy recipes torn out of magazines which are continued on the reverse side of the page. (Of course, if you prefer to spend time copying those recipes onto recipe cards instead of actually cooking, go right ahead.)

"Life is too short to stuff a mushroom."
—*Shirley Conran*

Spouses

Q: What do you recommend doing with other people's clutter that gets in your way, like spouse's junk?

A: It depends on the spouse and on the junk. But a good general rule is to designate an area where it's OK for the messy spouse to dump their stuff (or for you to put it there if he or she leaves it somewhere else). For example, my husband (a.k.a. "the most disorganized man in the world") has a small home office that we have agreed can be used as his perpetual dumping ground, as long as he keeps the door closed at all times. The Pit, as we call it, has been quite a marriage-saver; it gives me a place to put any clutter that Henry leaves elsewhere. When the Pit gets too cluttered for him to work in (a situation that seems to arise about twice a year), he spends several hours decluttering to his own satisfaction.

If designating a Pit room isn't an option, use a closet or even a corner of a room (use a folding screen as a divider; you can always paint it to look like a neat room). The most important thing is to be realistic about the likelihood that your spouse probably isn't going to change, so communication and compromise are essential. It's also vital to establish mutually agreed upon rules and standards, e.g., you agree not to discard each others' stuff without the owner's permission. (For resources on the topic of living with a clutterer, see Appendix B.)

"The only time a woman really succeeds in changing a man is when he is a baby." —*Natalie Wood*

Teenagers

Q: What can I do to help my teenage daughter unclutter her room?

A: First, identify her activity areas. For example, she probably needs areas for doing schoolwork, storing supplies, and keeping clothing and accessories. Have her use the decluttering steps described in Chapter Five to purge excess items from any area that is bogged down with clutter. Just don't throw out her stuff for her (unless it is starting to resemble another type of life form). Discarding without discussing may be regarded as "dissing," which eventually can cause more chaos in your relationship than clutter.

Make it easy for her to keep things in a semblance of order by setting up a simple categorizing system. You can even use laundry baskets in different colors for sorting clothes, papers, toiletries, or any other clutter sources.

Appendices

Which Records to Keep and for How Long

● ●

According to the Internal Revenue Service, records such as receipts, canceled checks, and other documents that prove an item of income or a deduction appearing on your return should be kept until the statute of limitations expires for that return. Usually this is three years from the date the return was due or filed, or two years from the date the tax was paid, whichever is later. However, there is no period of limitations when a return is false or fraudulent or when no return is filed. For more details, request Publication 552 from the IRS by calling (703) 487-4608 or visiting their Web site at www.irs.gov.

The following list is to be used as a guideline only. Please consult your legal counsel or tax adviser for professional advice.

Record Type	How Long to Keep It
AUTOMOBILE	
Accident	Until claims are settled
Gas and parking	For tax deductions, 3 years
Insurance	Until policy expires/claims settled
Purchase	Until car is sold
Payments	Until car is sold
Registration	Until car is sold
Repairs	Until car is sold

Record Type	How Long to Keep It
AUTOMOBILE *(CONTINUED)*	
Title	Until car is sold
Warranties	Warranty expiration or claims settled
BANK	
ATM slips	Until confirmation statement
Check register	3 years
Checks	3 years, if tax related
Checking statements	7 years
Deposit slips	Until confirmation statement
Passbook	Until account is closed
Savings: statement	Until account is closed
BILLS	
Charge Account: statements	For tax purposes, 3 years
Credit voucher	Until confirmed on account statement
Installment payments	Until loan is repaid
Mortgages/rent	Until home is sold or lease expires
Receipts/bill stubs	For tax purposes, 3 years
CORRESPONDENCE	
Legal	Permanently
Personal	Optional
DENTAL/ORTHODONTIC	
Bills	For tax purposes, 3 years or until claims are settled
Clinical	Permanent

Record Type	How Long to Keep It
EMPLOYMENT RECORDS	
Contracts	Permanent
Correspondence	Permanent
Pay stubs	3 years
Recommendations	Permanent
W-2s	Permanent
FAMILY RECORDS	
Birth certificate	Permanent
Children's grades	Until graduation
Diploma	Permanent
Divorce settlement	Permanent
Jury service	Until next duty
Marriage certificate	Permanent
Military service	Permanent
Naturalization papers	Permanent
Passport	Until receipt of renewed passport
Pet papers	For life of pet
Social Security	Permanent
Travel incentive award	Until expiration
Trust document	Until expiration or settlement of all claims
Will	Until settlement of all claims
FINANCIAL	
Annuities	Until account is closed
Appraisal	Until sale
Brokerage account	Until account is closed
Certificate of deposit	Until account is closed
Disability insurance	Until cancelled or settlement of all claims

Record Type	How Long to Keep It
FINANCIAL *(CONTINUED)*	
Life insurance	Permanent
Mutual funds	Until account is closed
Pensions/IRA	Until account is closed
Stock certificates, bond	Until sale
TAXES	
Federal income tax forms	Permanent
State income tax forms	Permanent
HOUSEHOLD	
Appraisal	Until house is sold
Closing documents	Permanent
Deed/title	Until house is sold
Homeowner's insurance	Until expiration
Improvements	Until house is sold
Inventory of valuables	Permanent
Ownership manual	For life of appliance
Repairs	For tax purposes, 3 years
Property taxes	Until house is sold
Title insurance	Until house is sold
Warranties	Until expiration
MEDICAL	
Allergy	Permanent
Bills	For tax purposes, 3 years or until claims are settled
Hospitalization	Permanent
Immunization schedule	Permanent
Medication	Permanent

Resources for Additional Help in Conquering Clutter

Books

Aslett, Don. *Clutter's Last Stand.* 1985, Writer's Digest Books.

Culp, Stephanie. *How to Conquer Clutter.* 1989, Writer's Digest Books.

Felton, Sandra. *When You Live with a Messie.* 1994, Revell.

Felton, Sandra. *The Messies Superguide.* 2nd ed. 1991, Revell.

Goldsmith, Olivia, and Amy Fine Collins. *Simple Isn't Easy.* 1995, Harper-Paperbacks.

Kanarck, Lisa. *Organizing Your Home Office for Success,* 2nd ed. 1998, Blakely Press.

Morgenstern, Julie. *Organizing from the Inside Out.* 1998, Henry Holt and Co.

Schechter, Harriet. *Conquering Chaos at Work: Strategies for Managing Disorganization and the People Who Cause It.* 2000, Fireside/Simon & Schuster.

Schechter, Harriet, and Vicki T. Gibbs. *More Time for Sex: The Organizing Guide for Busy Couples.* 2nd ed. 2000, iUniverse.com.

Schlenger, Sunny, and Roberta Roesch. *How to Be Organized in Spite of Yourself.* 2nd ed. 1999, Signet.

Silver, Susan. *Organized to Be Your Best!* 4th ed. 2000, Adams-Hall.

Organizations and Services

Association of Records Managers and Administrators (800) 422-2762
www.arma.org
Record-keeping guidelines resources.

Creative Memories (800) 468-9335

www.creativememories.com

Scrapbooking and photo album resources and services.

www.letgoclutter.com

Web site created for readers of *Let Go of Clutter*, offering updated tips and
resources on the topic of clutter control.

Messies Anonymous (800) 637-7292

www.messies.com

Support and resources for clutter sufferers of all kinds, including people
with Packrat Syndrome.

OrganizedU (877) 859-1585 (toll-free)

www.organizedu.com

Services and resources both for organizers and people who are seeking
organizing assistance.

For Additional Help

● ●

Since 1986, Harriet Schechter has been helping individuals, businesses, and nonprofit institutions get and stay organized through her customized consulting programs and workshops. In 1988 she began teaching the "Letting Go of Clutter" workshop series for the San Diego Learning Annex, and it has become one of their most popular ongoing courses.

Harriet provides answers to clutter questions via her advice column on The Miracle Worker's Web site: www.MiracleOrganizing.com. For information about her consulting and presentation programs, please contact Harriet through the Web site, or write to her c/o The Miracle Worker Organizing Service, PMB 199, 3368 Governor Drive, San Diego, California 92122.

Harriet also offers training for people who are interested in becoming professional organizers. Information on how to become a professional organizer can be obtained via the Web site, or by sending a stamped, self-addressed business envelope to the above address.

Index

Page numbers in **bold** indicate locations of worksheets.

About the Author

● ●

HARRIET SCHECHTER, a.k.a. "The Miracle Worker," is an internationally acclaimed pioneer in the professional organizing industry. She founded her San Diego-based company, The Miracle Worker Organizing Service, in 1986, and has taught the Learning Annex's popular "Letting Go of Clutter" workshop regularly since 1988.